AFLOAT ON THE OHIO

Shawnee Classics
A Series of Classic Regional Reprints for the Midwest

Afloat on the Ohio

AN HISTORICAL PILGRIMAGE OF A THOUSAND MILES IN A SKIFF, FROM REDSTONE TO CAIRO

BY

REUBEN GOLD THWAITES

Secretary of the State Historical Society of Wisconsin, Editor of "The Jesuit Relations," Author of "The Colonies, 1492-1750," "Historic Waterways," "The Story of Wisconsin," "Our Cycling Tour in England," etc., etc.

Southern Illinois University Press
Carbondale and Edwardsville

First published 1897 by Way & Williams
New edition published 1999 by Southern Illinois University
    Press
All rights reserved
Printed in the United States of America
02 01 00 99 4 3 2 1

Library of Congress Cataloging-in-Publication Data
Thwaites, Reuben Gold, 1853–1913.
    Afloat on the Ohio : an historical pilgrimage of a thousand
miles in a skiff, from Redstone to Cairo / by Reuben Gold
Thwaites.
        p.   cm. — (Shawnee classics)
    Originally published: Way & Williams, 1897.
    Includes bibliographical references and index.
    1. Ohio River—Description and travel. 2. Ohio River
Region—Social life and customs. 3. Thwaites, Reuben Gold,
1853–1913—Journeys—Ohio River. 4. Skiffs—Ohio
River—History—19th century. I. Title. II. Series.
    F519.T54 1999
    917.704'31—dc21   98-51306
    ISBN 0-8093-2268-4 (pbk. : alk. paper)   CIP

The paper used in this publication meets the minimum
requirements of American National Standard for Information
Sciences—Permanence of Paper for Printed Library Materials,
ANSI Z39.48-1984. ♾

CONTENTS.

CONTENTS

CONTENTS

PUBLISHER'S NOTE

American nineteenth-century travel literature provides fascinating glimpses into the lives of ordinary people and into the history of the nation's settlement. Reuben Gold Thwaites's *Afloat on the Ohio* is a fine example of the genre, rich in Ohio River personalities, legends, and history as seen through Thwaites's eyes.

Journalist, librarian, and editor Reuben Gold Thwaites was born in Dorchester, Massachusetts, in 1853. At the age of thirteen he moved to Wisconsin, where in 1876 he became managing editor of the *Wisconsin State Journal*. In 1887 Thwaites was appointed secretary of the Wisconsin State Historical Society, and it is during his tenure that the Society became an important center for historical research. A prolific editor and writer, Thwaites edited an annual volume of the Society's *Proceedings* in addition to *Jesuit Relations* and *Allied Documents* (1896–1901, 73 volumes), *Original Journals of the Lewis and Clark Expedition* (1904–5, 8 volumes), and *Early Western Travels* (1904–7, 32 volumes of annotated reprints). He is the author of numerous books including *France in America*, 1497–1763 (1905) and *Wisconsin: The Americanization of a French Settlement* (1908). Thwaites died in Madison, Wisconsin, in 1913.

Afloat on the Ohio was originally printed in October 1897 by the Blakeley Printing Company for Way & Williams of Chicago. It was subsequently published in another edition (1903), which in turn was reprinted in facsimile by Ayer Company Publishers in 1975 and retitled *On the Storied Ohio*. The Southern Illinois University Press edition is a reprinting of the original 1897 edition.

PREFACE.

THERE were four of us pilgrims—my Wife, our Boy of ten and a half years, the Doctor, and I. My object in going—the others went for the outing—was to gather "local color" for work in Western history. The Ohio River was an important factor in the development of the West. I wished to know the great waterway intimately in its various phases,—to see with my own eyes what the borderers saw; in imagination, to redress the pioneer stage, and repeople it.

A motley company have here performed their parts: Savages of the mound-building age, rearing upon these banks curious earthworks for archæologists of the nineteenth century to puzzle over; Iroquois war-parties, silently swooping upon sleeping villages of the Shawanese, and in noisy glee returning to the New York lakes, laden with spoils and captives; La Salle, prince of French explorers and coureurs de bois, standing at the Falls of

the Ohio, and seeking to fathom the geographical mysteries of the continent; French and
English fur-traders, in bitter contention for
the patronage of the red man; borderers of
the rival nations, shedding each other's blood
in protracted partisan wars; surveyors like
Washington and Boone and the McAfees, clad
in fringed hunting-shirts and leathern leggings,
mapping out future states; hardy frontiers-
men, fighting, hunting, or farming, as occasion
demanded; George Rogers Clark, descending
the river with his handful of heroic Virginians
to win for the United States the great Northwest, and for himself the laurels of fame;
the Marietta pilgrims, beating Revolutionary
swords into Ohio plowshares; and all that
succeeding tide of immigrants from our own
Atlantic coast and every corner of Europe,
pouring down the great valley to plant powerful commonwealths beyond the mountains.
A richly-varied panorama of life passes before
us as we contemplate the glowing story of
the Ohio.

In making our historical pilgrimage we might
more easily have "steamboated" the river, —
to use a verb in local vogue; but, from the
deck of a steamer, scenes take on a different

aspect than when viewed from near the level
of the flood; for a passenger by such a craft,
the vistas of a winding stream change so rapidly that he does not realize how it seemed to
the canoeist or flatboatman of old; and there
are too many modern distractions about such
a mode of progress. To our minds, the manner of our going should as nearly as possible
be that of the pioneer himself—hence our skiff,
and our nightly camp in primitive fashion.

The trip was successful, whatever the point
of view. Physically, those six weeks "Afloat
on the Ohio" were a model outing—at times
rough, to be sure, but exhilarating, health-
giving, brain-inspiring. The Log of the "Pilgrim" seeks faintly to outline our experiences,
but no words can adequately describe the
wooded hill-slopes which day by day girt us
in; the romantic ravines which corrugate the
rim of the Ohio's basin; the beautiful islands
which stud the glistening tide; the great affluents which, winding down for a thousand
miles, from the Blue Ridge, the Cumberland,
and the Great Smoky, pour their floods into
the central stream; the giant trees—sycamores, pawpaws, cork elms, catalpas, walnuts,
and what not—which everywhere are in view

in this woodland world; the strange and lovely
flowers we saw; the curious people we met,
black and white, and the varieties of dialect
which caught our ear; the details of our
charming gypsy life, ashore and afloat, during
which we were conscious of the red blood
tingling through our veins, and, alert to the
whisperings of Nature, were careless of the
workaday world, so far away,—simply glad to
be alive.

For the better understanding of the numerous historical references in the Log, I have
thought it well to present in the Appendix
a brief sketch of the settlement of the Ohio
Valley. To this Appendix, as a preliminary
reading, I invite those who may care to follow
" Pilgrim" and her crew upon their long journey from historic Redstone down to the Father
of Waters.

A selected list of Journals of previous travelers down the Ohio, has been added, for the
benefit of students of the social and economic
history of this important gateway to the continental interior.

R. G. T.

MADISON, WIS., October, 1897.

AFLOAT ON THE OHIO

CHAPTER I.

ON THE MONONGAHELA—THE OVER-MOUNTAIN
PATH—REDSTONE OLD FORT—THE YOUGH-
IOGHENY—BRADDOCK'S DEFEAT.

IN CAMP NEAR CHARLEROI, PA., Friday,
May 4.—Pilgrim, built for the glassy lakes
and smooth-flowing rivers of Wisconsin, had
suffered unwonted indignities in her rough
journey of a thousand miles in a box-car. But
beyond a leaky seam or two, which the Doctor had righted with clouts and putty, and
some ugly scratches which were only paint-
deep, she was in fair trim as she gracefully lay
at the foot of the Brownsville shipyard this
morning and received her lading.

There were spectators in abundance.
Brownsville, in the olden day, had seen many
an expedition set out from this spot for the

1

grand tour of the Ohio, but not in the personal recollection of any in this throng of idlers, for the era of the flatboat and pirogue now belongs to history. Our expedition is a revival, and therein lies novelty. However, the historic spirit was not evident among our visitors—railway men, coal miners loafing out the duration of a strike, shipyard hands lying in wait for busier times, small boys blessed with as much leisure as curiosity, and that wonder of wonders, a bashful newspaper reporter. Their chief concern centered in the query, how Pilgrim could hold that goodly heap of luggage and still have room to spare for four passengers? It became evident that her capacity is akin to that of the magician's bag.

"A dandy skiff, gents!" said the foreman of the shipyard, as we settled into our seats— the Doctor bow, I stroke, with W— and the Boy in the stern sheets. Having in silence critically watched us for a half hour, seated on a capstan, his red flannel shirt rolled up to his elbows, and well-corded chest and throat bared to wind and weather, this remark of the foreman was evidently the studied judgment of an expert. It was taken as such by the good-natured crowd, which, as we pushed off into the stream, lustily joined in a chorus of "Good-bye!" and "Good luck to yees, an' ye don't git th' missus drowndid 'fore ye git to Cairo!"

The current is slight on these lower reaches of the Monongahela. It comes down gayly enough from the West Virginia hills, over many a rapid, and through swirls and eddies in plenty, until Morgantown is reached; and then, settling into a more sedate course, is at Brownsville finally converted into a mere mill-pond, by the back-set of the four slack-water dams between there and Pittsburg. This means solid rowing for the first sixty miles of our journey, with a current scarcely percep-tible.

The thought of it suggests lunch. At the mouth of Redstone Creek, a mile below Dun-lap Creek, our port of departure, we turn in to a shaly beach at the foot of a wooded slope, in semi-rusticity, and fortify the inner man.

A famous spot, this Redstone Creek. Be-tween its mouth and that of Dunlap's was made, upon the site of extensive Indian forti-fication mounds, the first English agricultural settlement west of the Alleghanies. It is un-safe to establish dates for first discoveries, or

for first settlements. The wanderers who,
first of all white men, penetrated the fastnesses of the wilderness were mostly of the
sort who left no documentary traces behind
them. It is probable, however, that the first
Redstone settlement was made as early as
1750, the year following the establishment of
the Ohio Company, which had been chartered
by the English crown and given a half-million
acres of land west of the mountains and south
of the Ohio River, provided it established
thereon a hundred families within seven years.

"Redstone Old Fort"—the name had ref-
erence to the aboriginal earthworks—played
a part in the Fort Necessity and Braddock
campaigns and in later frontier wars; and,
being the western terminus of the over-mountain road known at various historic periods as
Nemacolin's Path, Braddock's Road, and
Cumberland Pike, was for many years the
chief point of departure for Virginia expeditions down the Ohio River. Washington, who
had large landed interests on the Ohio, knew
Redstone well; and here George Rogers Clark
set out (1778) upon flatboats, with his rough-
and-ready Virginia volunteers, to capture the
country north of the Ohio for the American

arms—one of the least known, but most momentous conquests in history.

Early in the nineteenth century, Redstone became Brownsville. But, whether as Redstone or Brownsville, it was, in its day, like most "jumping off" places on the edge of civilization, a veritable Sodom. Wrote good old John Pope, in his Journal of 1790, and in the same strain scores of other veracious chroniclers: "At this Place we were detained about a Week, experiencing every Disgust which Rooks and Harpies could excite." Here thrived extensive yards in which were built flatboats, arks, keel boats, and all that miscellaneous collection of water craft which, with their roisterly crews, were the life of the Ohio before the introduction of steam rendered vessels of deeper draught essential; whereupon much of the shipping business went down the river to better stages of water, first to Pittsburg, thence to Wheeling, and to Steubenville.

All that is of the past. Brownsville is still a busy corner of the world, though of a different sort, with all its romance gone. To the student of Western history, Brownsville will always be a shrine—albeit a smoky, dusty shrine, with the smell of lubricators and the

clang of hammers, and much talk thereabout
of the glories of Mammon.

The Monongahela is a characteristic mountain trough. From an altitude of four or five
hundred feet, the country falls in sharp steeps
to a narrow alluvial bench, and then a broad
beach of shale and pebble; the slopes are
broken, here and there, where deep, shadowy
ravines come winding down, bearing muddy
contributions to the greater flood. The higher
hills are crowned with forest trees, the lower
ofttimes checkered with brown fields, recently
planted, and rows of vines trimmed low to
stakes, as in the fashion of the Rhine. The
stream, though still majestic in its sweep, is
henceforth a commercial slack-water, lined
with noisy, grimy, matter-of-fact manufacturing towns, for the most part literally abutting
one upon the other all of the way down to
Pittsburg, and fast defiling the once picturesque
banks with the gruesome offal of coal mines
and iron plants. Surprising is the density of
settlement along the river. Often, four or five
full-fledged cities are at once in view from our
boat, the air is thick with sooty smoke belched
from hundreds of stacks, the ear is almost

deafened with the whirr and roar and bang of milling industries.

Tipples of bituminous coal-shafts are ever in sight—begrimed scaffolds of wood and iron, arranged for dumping the product of the mines into both barges and railway cars. Either bank is lined with railways, in sight of which we shall almost continually float, all the way down to Cairo, nearly eleven hundred miles away. At each tipple is a miners' hamlet; a row of cottages or huts, cast in a common mold, either unpainted, or bedaubed with that cheap, ugly red with which one is familiar in railway bridges and rural barns. Sometimes these huts, though in the mass dreary enough, are kept in neat repair; but often are they sadly out of elbows—pigs and children promiscuously at their doors, paneless sash stuffed with rags, unsightly litter strewn around, misery stamped on every feature of the homeless tenements. Dreariest of all is a deserted mining village, and there are many such—the shaft having been worked out, or an unquenchable subterranean fire left to smolder in neglect. Here the tipple has fallen into creaking decrepitude; the cabins are without windows or doors—these having been taken to some newer hamlet; ridge-poles are sunken, chimneys tottering; soot covers the gaunt bones, which for all the world are like a row of skeletons, perched high, and grinning down at you in their misery; while the black offal of the pit, covering deep the original beauty of the once green slope, is in its turn being veiled with climbing weeds—such is Nature's haste, when untrammeled, to heal the scars wrought by man.

A mile or two below Charleroi is Lock No. 4, the first of the quartet of obstructions between Brownsville and Pittsburg. We are encamped a mile below the dam, in a cozy little willowed nook; a rod behind our ample tent rises the face of an alluvial terrace, occupied by a grain-field, running back for an hundred yards to the hills, at the base of which is a railway track. Across the river, here some two hundred and fifty yards wide, the dark, rocky bluffs, slashed with numerous ravines, ascend sharply from the flood; at the quarried base, a wagon road and the customary railway; and upon the stony beach, two or three rough shelter-tents, housing the Black Diamond Brass Band, of Monongahela City, out on a week's picnic to while away the period of the strike.

It was seven o'clock when we struck camp, and our frugal repast was finished by lantern-light. The sun sets early in this narrow trough through the foothills of the Laurel range.

McKEESPORT, PA., Saturday, May 5th.— Out there on the beach, near Charleroi, with the sail for an awning, Pilgrim had been converted into a boudoir for the Doctor, who, snuggled in his sleeping-bag, emitted an occasional snore—echoes from the Land of Nod. W— and our Boy of ten summers, on their canvas folding-cots, were peacefully oblivious of the noises of the night, and needed the kiss of dawn to rouse them. But for me, always a light sleeper, and as yet unused to our airy bedroom, the crickets chirruped through the long watches.

Two or three freighters passed in the night, with monotonous swish-swish and swelling wake. It arouses something akin to awe, this passage of a steamer's wake upon the beach, a dozen feet from the door of one's tent. First, the water is sucked down, leaving for a moment a wet streak of sand or gravel, a dozen

feet in width; in quick succession come heavy,
booming waves, running at an acute angle with
the shore, breaking at once into angry foam,
and wasting themselves far up on the strand,
for a few moments making bedlam with any
driftwood which chances to have made lodg-
ment there. When suddenly awakened by
this boisterous turmoil, the first thought is
that a dam has broken and a flood is at hand;
but, by the time you rise upon your elbow, the
scurrying uproar lessens, and gradually dies
away along a more distant shore.

We were slow in getting off this morning.
But the dense fog had been loath to lift; and
at first the stove smoked badly, until we discovered and removed the source of trouble.
This stove is an ingenious contrivance of the
Doctor's—a box of sheet-iron, of slight weight,
so arranged as to be folded into an incredibly
small space; a vast improvement for cooking
purposes over an open camp-fire, which Pilgrim's crew know, from long experience in far
distant fields, to be a vexation to eyes and soul.

Coaling hamlets more or less deserted were
frequent this morning—unpainted, windowless, ragged wrecks. At the inhabited mining
villages, either close to the strand or well up

on hillside ledges, idle men were everywhere about. Women and boys and girls were stockingless and shoeless, and often dirty to a degree. But, when conversed with, we found them independent, respectful, and self-respecting folk. Occasionally I would, for the mere sake of meeting these workaday brothers of ours, with canteen slung on shoulder, climb the steep flight of stairs cut in the clay bank, and on reaching the terrace inquire for drinking water, talking familiarly with the folk who came to meet me at the well-curb.

There are old-fashioned Dutch ovens in nearly every yard, a few chickens, and often a shed for the cow, that is off on her daily climb over the neighboring hills. Through the black pall of shale, a few vegetables struggle feebly to the light; in the corners of the palings, are hollyhocks and four-o'clocks; and, on window-sills, rows of battered tin cans, resplendent in blue and yellow labels, are the homes of verbenas and geraniums, in sickly bloom. Now and then, a back door in the dreary block is distinguished by an arbored trellis bearing a grape-vine, and furnishing for the weary housewife a shady kitchen, *al fresco*. As a rule, however, there is little attempt to better the homeless shelter furnished by the corporation.

We restocked with provisions at Mononga-hela City, a smart, newish town, and at Elizabeth, old and dingy. It was at Elizabeth, then Elizabethtown, that travelers from the Eastern States, over the old Philadelphia Road, chiefly took boat for the Ohio—the Virginians still clinging to Redstone, as the terminus of the Braddock Road. Elizabethtown, in flat-boat days, was the seat of a considerable boat-building industry, its yards in time turning out steamboats for the New Orleans trade, and even sea-going sailing craft; but, to-day, coal barges are the principal output of her decaying shipyards.

By this time, the duties of our little ship's company are well defined. W— supervises the cuisine, most important of all offices; the Doctor is chief navigator, assistant cook, and hewer of wood; it falls to my lot to purchase supplies, to be carrier of water, to pitch tent and make beds, and, while breakfast is being cooked, to dismantle the camp and, so far as may be, to repack Pilgrim; the Boy collects driftwood, wipes dishes, and helps at what he can—while all hands row or paddle through the livelong day, as whim or need dictates.

Lock No. 3, at Walton, necessitated a portage of the load, over the left bank. It is a steep, rocky climb, and the descent on the lower side, strewn with stone chips, destructive to shoe-leather. The Doctor and I let Pilgrim herself down with a long rope, over a shallow spot in the apron of the dam.

At six o'clock a camping-ground for the night became desirable. We were fortunate, last evening, to find a bit of rustic country in which to pitch our tent; but all through this afternoon both banks of the river were lined with village after village, city after city, scarcely a garden patch between them—Wilson, Coal Valley, Lostock, Glassport, Dravosburg, and a dozen others not recorded on our map, which bears date of 1882. The sun was setting behind the rim of the river basin, when we reached the broad mouth of the Youghiogheny (pr. Yock-i-o-gai-ny), which is implanted with a cluster of iron-mill towns, of which McKeesport is the center. So far as we could see down the Monongahela, the air was thick with the smoke of glowing chimneys, and the pulsating whang of steel-making plants and rolling-mills made the air tremble. The view up the "Yough" was more inviting; so, with oars and paddle firmly set, we turned off our course and lustily pulled against the strong current of the tributary. A score or two of house-boats lay tied to the McKeesport shore or were bolstered high upon the beach; a fleet of Yough steamers had their noses to the wharf; a half-dozen fishermen were setting nets; and, high over all, with lofty spans of iron cobweb, several railway and wagon bridges spanned the gliding stream.

It was a mile and a half up the Yough before we reached the open country; and then only the rapidly-gathering dusk drove us ashore, for on near approach the prospect was not pleasing. Finally settling into this damp, shallow pocket in the shelving bank, we find broad-girthed elms and maples screening us from all save the river front, the high bank in the rear fringed with blue violets which emit a delicious odor, backed by a field of waving corn stretching off toward heavily-wooded hills. Our supper cooked and eaten by lantern-light, we vote ourselves as, after all, serenely content out here in the starlight—at peace with the world, and very close to Nature's heart.

There come to us, on the cool evening breeze, faint echoes of the never-ceasing clang of McKeesport iron mills, down on the Monongahela shore. But it is not of these we talk, lounging in the welcome warmth of the camp-fire; it is of the age of romance, a hundred and forty odd years ago, when Major Washington and Christopher Gist, with famished horses, floundered in the ice hereabout, upon their famous midwinter trip to Fort Le Bœuf; when the "Forks of the Yough" became the extreme outpost of Western advance, with all the accompanying horrors of frontier war; and later, when McKeesport for a time rivaled Redstone and Elizabethtown as a center for boat-building and a point of departure for the Ohio.

PITTSBURG, Sunday, May 6th.—Many of the trees are already in full leaf. The trillium is fading. We are in the full tide of early summer, up here in the mountains, and our long journey of six weeks is southward and toward the plain. The lower Ohio may soon be a bake-oven, and the middle of June will be upon us before far-away Cairo is reached.

It behooves us to be up and doing. The river, flowing by our door, is an ever-pressing invitation to be onward; it stops not for Sunday, nor ever stops—and why should we, mere drift upon the passing tide?

There was a smart thunder-shower during breakfast, followed by a cool, cloudy morning. At eleven o'clock Pilgrim was laden. A southeastern breeze ruffled the waters of the Yough, and for the first time the Doctor ordered up the sail, with W— at the sheet. It was not long before Pilgrim had the water "singing at her prow." With a rush, we flew past the factories, the house-boats, and the shabby street-ends of McKeesport, out into the Monongahela, where, luckily, the wind still held.

At McKeesport, the hills on the right are of a relatively low altitude, smooth and well rounded. It was here that Braddock, in his slow progress toward Fort Duquesne, first crossed the Monongahela, to the wide, level bottom on the left bank. He had found the inner country to the right of the river and below the Yough too rough and hilly for his march, hence had turned back toward the Monongahela, fording the river to take advantage of the less difficult bottom. Some

four miles below this first crossing, hills reap-
proach the left bank, till the bottom ceases;
the right thenceforth becomes the more favorable side for marching.   With great pomp, he
recrossed the Monongahela just below the
point where Turtle Creek enters from the east.
Within a hillside ravine, but a hundred yards
inland, the brilliant column fell into an ambuscade of Indians and French half-breeds,
suffering that heart-sickening defeat which will
ever live as one of the most tragic events in
American history.

The noisy iron-manufacturing town of Braddock now occupies the site of Braddock's defeat.   Not far from the old ford stretches the
great dam of Lock No. 2, which we portaged,
with the usual difficulties of steep, stony banks.
Braddock is but eight miles across country
from Pittsburg, although twelve by river.   We
have, all the way down, an almost constant
succession of iron and steel-making towns,
chief among them Homestead, on the left
bank, seven miles above Pittsburg.   The great
strike of July, 1892, with its attendant horrors,
is a lurid chapter in the story of American industry.   With shuddering interest, we view the
famous great bank of ugly slag at the base of

2

the steel mills, where the barges housing the Pinkerton guards were burned by the mob.

To-day, the Homesteaders are enjoying their Sunday afternoon outing along the town shore—nurses pushing baby carriages, self-absorbed lovers holding hands upon riverside benches, merry-makers rowing in skiffs or crossing the river in crowded ferries; the electric cars, following either side of the stream as far down as Pittsburg, crowded to suffocation with gayly-attired folk. They look little like rioters; yet it seems but the other day when Homestead men and women and children were hysterically reveling in atrocities akin to those of the Paris commune.

Approaching Pittsburg, the high steeps are everywhere crowded with houses—great masses of smoke-color, dotted all over with white shades and sparkling windows, which seem, in the gray afternoon, to be ten thousand eyes coldly staring down at Pilgrim and her crew from all over the flanking hillsides.

Lock No. 1, the last barrier between us and the Ohio, is a mile or two up the Mononga-hela, with warehouses and manufacturing plants closely hemming it in on either side. A portage, unaided, appears to be impossible

here, and we resolve to lock through. But it
is Sunday, and the lock is closed. Above, a
dozen down-going steamboats are moored to
the shore, waiting for midnight and the re-
sumption of business; while below, a similar
line of ascending boats is awaiting the close
of the day of rest. Pilgrim, however, cannot
hang up at the levee with any comfort to her
crew; it is necessary, with evening at hand,
and a thunder-storm angrily rising over the
Pittsburg hills, to get out of this grimy pool,
flanked about with iron and coal yards, chimney stacks, and a forest of shipping, and to
quickly seek the open country lower down on
the Ohio. The lock-keepers appreciated our
situation. Two or three sturdy, courteous
men helped us carry our cargo, by an intricate
official route, over coils of rope and chains,
over lines of shafting, and along dizzy walks
overhanging the yawning basin; while the
Doctor, directed to a certain chute in mid-
stream, took unladen Pilgrim over the great
dam, with a wild swoop which made our eyes
swim to witness from the lock.

We had laboriously been rowing on slack-
water, all the way from Brownsville, with the
help of an hour's sail this morning; whereas,

now that we were in the strong current below
the dam, we had but to gently paddle to glide
swiftly on our way. A hundred steamers,
more or less, lay closely packed with their
bows upon the right, or principal city wharf.
It was raining at last, and we donned our
storm wraps. No doubt yellow Pilgrim, —
thought hereabout to be a frail craft for these
waters, — her crew all poncho-clad, slipping
silently through the dark water swishing at their
sterns, was a novelty to the steamboat men, for
they leaned lazily over their railings, the officers
on the upper deck, engineers and roustabouts
on the lower, and watched us curiously.

Our period of elation was brief. Black
storm-clouds, jagged and portentous, were
scurrying across the sky; and by the time we
had reached the forks, where the Monongahela, in the heart of the city, joins forces with
the Alleghany, Pilgrim was being buffeted
about on a chop sea produced by cross currents
and a northwest gale. She can weather an
ordinary storm, but this experience was too
much for her. When a passing steamer threw
out long lines of frothy waves to add to the
disturbance, they broke over our gunwales;
and W— with the coffee pot and the Boy

with a tin basin were hard pushed to keep the
water below the thwarts.

Seeking the friendly shelter of a house-boat,
of which there were scores tied to the left
bank, we trusted our drenched luggage to the
care of its proprietor, placed Pilgrim in a snug
harbor hard by, and, hurrying up a steep flight
of steps leading from the levee to the terrace
above, found a suburban hotel just as its office
clock struck eight.

Across the Ohio, through the blinding storm,
the dark outlines of Pittsburg and Allegheny
City are spangled with electric lamps which
throw toward us long, shimmering lances of
light, in which the mighty stream, gray, mysterious, tempest-tossed, is seen to be surging
onward with majestic sweep.   Upon its bosom
we are to be borne for a thousand miles.   Our
introduction has been unpropitious; it is to be
hoped that on further acquaintance we may
be better pleased with La Belle Rivière.

CHAPTER II.

BEAVER RIVER, Monday, May 7th.—We have to-day rowed and paddled under a cloudless sky, but in the teeth of frequent squalls, with heavy waves freely dashing their spray upon us. At such times a goodly current, aided by numerous wing-dams, appears of little avail; for, when we rested upon our oars, Pilgrim would be unmercifully driven up stream. Thus it has been an almost continual fight to make progress, and our five-and-twenty miles represent a hard day's work.

We were overloaded, that was certain; so we stopped at Chartier, three miles down the river from Pittsburg, and sent on our portly bag of conventional traveling clothes by express to Cincinnati, where we intend stopping for a day. This leaves us in our rough boating costumes for all the smaller towns *en route*. What we may lose in possible social embarrassments, we gain in lightened cargo.

22

Here at the mouth of Chartier's Creek was
"Chartier's Old Town" of a century and a
third ago; a straggling, unkempt Indian village
then, but at least the banks were lovely, and
the rolling distances clothed with majestic
trees.   To-day, these creek banks, connected
with numerous iron bridges, are the dumping-
ground for cinders, slag, rubbish of every degree of foulness; the bare hillsides are crowded
with the ugly dwellings of iron-workers; the
atmosphere is thick with smoke.

Washington, one of the greatest land speculators of his time, owned over 32,000 acres
along the Ohio.   He held a patent from Lord
Dunmore, dated July 5, 1775, for nearly 3,000
acres lying about the mouth of this stream.
In accordance with the free-and-easy habit of
trans-Alleghany pioneers, ten men squatted on
the tract, greatly to the indignation of the
Father of his Country, who in 1784 brought
against them a successful suit for ejectment.
Twelve years later, more familiar with this
than with most of his land grants, he sold it
to a friend for $12,000.

Just below Chartier are the picturesque
McKee's Rocks, where is the first riffle in the
Ohio.   We "take" it with a swoop, the white-

capped waves dancing about us in a miniature
rapid. Then we are in the open country, and
for the first time find what the great river is
like. The character of the banks, for some
distance below Pittsburg, differs from that of
the Monongahela. The hills are lower, less
precipitous, more graceful. There is a delightful roundness of mass and shade. Beautiful villas occupy commanding situations on
hillsides and hilltops; we catch glimpses of
spires and cupolas, singly or in groups, peeping
above the trees; and now and then a pretty
suburban railway station. The railways upon
either bank are built on neat terraces, and, far
from marring the scene, agreeably give life to
it; now and then, three such terraces are to
be traced, one above the other, against the
dark background of wood and field—the lower
and upper devoted to rival railway lines, the
central one to the common way. The mouths
of the beautiful tributary ravines are crossed
either by graceful iron spans, which frame
charming undercut glimpses of sparkling water-
falls and deep tangles of moss and fern, or by
graceful stone arches draped with vines. There
are terraced vineyards, after the fashion of the
Rhineland, and the gentle arts of the florist

and the truck-gardener are much in evidence.
The winding river frequently sweeps at the
base of rocky escarpments, but upon one side
or the other there are now invariably bottom
lands—narrow on these upper reaches, but we
shall find them gradually widen and lengthen
as we descend.   The reaches are from four to
seven miles in length, but these, too, are to
lengthen in the middle waters.   Islands are
frequent, all day. The largest is Neville's, five
miles long and thickly strewn with villas and
market-gardens; still others are but long sand-
bars grown to willows, and but temporarily in
sight, for the stage of water is low just now,
not over seven feet in the channel.

Emerging from the immediate suburbs of
Pittsburg, the fields broaden, farmsteads are
occasionally to be seen nestled in the undula-
tions of the hills, woodlands become more
dense. There are, however, small rustic towns
in.plenty; we are seldom out of sight of these.
Climbing a steep clay slope on the left bank,
we visited one of them—Shousetown, fourteen
miles below the city. A sad-eyed, shabby
place, with the pipe line for natural gas sprawling hither and yon upon the surface of the
ground, except at the street crossings, where

a few inches of protecting earth have been laid upon it. The tariff levied by the gas company is ten cents per month for each light, and a dollar and a half for a cook-stove.

We passed, this afternoon, one of the most interesting historic points upon the river—the picturesque site of ancient Logstown, upon the summit of a low, steep ridge on the right bank, just below Economy, and eighteen miles from Pittsburg. Logstown was a Shawanese village as early as 1727-30, and already a notable fur-trading post when Conrad Weiser visited it in 1748. Washington and Gist stopped at ''Loggestown'' for five days on their visit to the French at Fort Le Bœuf, and several famous Indian treaties were signed there. A short distance below, Anthony Wayne's Western army was encamped during the winter of 1792-93, the place being then styled Legionville. In 1824 George Rapp founded in the neighborhood a German social-ist community, and this later settlement sur-vives to the present day in the thriving little rustic town of Economy.

At four o'clock we struck camp on a heavily-willowed shore, at the apex of the great north-

ern bend of the Ohio (25 miles).* Across the
river, on a broad level bottom, are the manufacturing towns of Rochester and Beaver,
divided by the Beaver River; in their rear,
well-rounded hills rise gracefully, checkered
with brown fields and woods in many shades
of green, in the midst of which the flowering
white dogwood rears its stately spray. Our
sloping willowed sand-beach, of a hundred feet
in width, is thick strewn with driftwood; back
of this a clay bank, eight feet sheer, and a
narrow bottom cut up with small fruit and
vegetable patches; the gardeners' neat frame
houses peeping from groves of apple, pear and
cherry, upon the flanking hillsides. A lofty
oil-well derrick surmounts the edge of the terrace a hundred yards below our camp. The
bushes and the ground round about the well
are black and slimy with crude petroleum, that
has escaped during the boring process, and the
air is heavy with its odor. We are upon the
edge of the far-stretching oil and gas-well re-

---

* Figures in parentheses, similarly placed throughout the
volume, indicate the meandered river mileage from Pittsburg,
according to the map of the Corps of Engineers, U. S. A.,
published in 1881. The actual mileage of the channel is a
trifle greater.

gion, and shall soon become familiar enough
with such sights and smells in the neighborhood of our nightly camps.

No sooner had Pilgrim been turned up against
a tree to dry, and a smooth sandy open chosen
for the camp, than the proprietor of the soil
appeared—a middling-sized, lanky man, with
a red face and a sandy goatee surmounting a
collarless white shirt all bestained with tobacco
juice. He inquired rather sharply concerning
us, but when informed of our innocent errand,
and that we should stay with him but the
night, he promptly softened, explaining that
the presence of marauding fishermen and houseboat folk was incompatible with gardening
for profit, and he would have none of them
touch upon his shore. As to us, we were welcome to stop throughout our pleasure, an invitation he reinforced by sitting upon a stump,
whittling vigorously meanwhile, and glibly
gossiping with the Doctor and me for a half-
hour, on crop conditions and the state of the
country—"bein' sociable like," he said, "an'
hav'n' nuth'n 'gin you folks, as knows what's
what, I kin see with half a eye!"

CHAPTER III.

Kneistly's Cluster, W. Va., Tuesday, May 8th.—We were off at a quarter past seven, and among the earliest shoppers in Rochester, on the east bank of the Beaver, where supplies were laid in for the day. This busy, prosperous-looking place bears little resemblance to the squalid Indian village which Gist found here in November, 1750. It was then the seat of Barney Curran, an Indian trader—the same Curran whom Washington, three years later, employed in the mission to Venango. But the smaller sister town of Beaver, on the lower side of the mouth,—or rather the western outskirts of Beaver a mile below the mouth, —has the most ancient history. On account of a ford across the Beaver, about where is now a slack-water dam, the neighborhood became of early importance to the French as a fur-trading center. With customary liberality toward the Indians, whom they assiduously cultivated, the French, in 1756, built for them, on this site, a substantial town, which the English indifferently called Sarikonk, Sohkon, King Beaver's Town, or Shingis Old Town. During the French and Indian War, the place was prominent as a rendezvous for the enemies of American borderers; numerous bloody forays were planned here, and hither were brought to be adopted into the tribes, or to be cruelly tortured, according to savage whim, many of the captives whose tales have made lurid the history of the Ohio Valley.

Passing Beaver River, the Ohio enters upon its grand sweep to the southwest. The wide uplands at once become more rustic, especially those of the left bank, which no longer is threaded by a railway, as heretofore all the way from Brownsville. The two ranges of undulating hills, some three hundred and fifty feet high, forming the rim of the basin, are about a half mile apart; while the river itself is perhaps a third of a mile in width, leaving narrow bottoms on alternate sides, as the stream in gentle curves rebounds from the rocky base of one hill to that of another. When winding about such a base, there is at this stage of the water a sloping, stony beach, some ten to twenty yards in width, from which ascends the sharp steep, for the most part heavily tree-clad—maples, birches, elms and oaks of goodly girth, the latter as yet in but half-leaf.   On the ''bottom side'' of the river, the alluvial terrace presents a sheer wall of clay rising from eight to a dozen feet above the beach, which is often thick-grown with willows, whose roots hold the soil from becoming too easy a prey to the encroaching current.   Syca-mores now begin to appear in the bottoms, although of less size than we shall meet below. Sometimes the little towns we see occupy a narrow and more or less rocky bench upon the hill side of the stream, but settlement is chiefly found upon the bottoms.

Shippingsport (32 miles), on the left bank, where we stopped this noon for eggs, butter, and fresh water, is on a narrow hill bench—a dry, woe-begone hamlet, side-tracked from the path of the world's progress.   While I was on shore, negotiating with the sleepy store-keeper, Pilgrim and her crew waited alongside the flatboat which serves as the town ferry. There they were visited by a breezy, red-faced young man, in a blue flannel shirt and a black

slouch hat, who was soon enough at his ease
to lie flat upon the ferry gunwale, his cheeks
supported by his hands, and talk to W— and
the Doctor as if they were old friends.   He
was a dealer in nitroglycerin cartridges, he
said, and pointed to a long, rakish-looking
skiff hard by, which bore a red flag at its prow.
"Ye see that?   Thet there red flag?   Well,
thet's the law on us glyser*een* fellers—over five
hundred poun's, two flags; un'er five hundred,
one flag.   I've two hundred and fifty, I have.
I tell yer th' steamboats steer clear o' me, an'
don' yer fergit it, neither; they jist give me a
wide berth, they do, yew bet!   'n' th' railroads,
they don' carry no glyser*een* cartridge, they
don't—all uv it by skiff, like yer see me goin'."

These cartridges, he explained, are dropped
into oil or gas wells whose owners are desirous
of accelerating the flow.   The cartridge, in
exploding, enlarges the hole, and often the
output of the well is at once increased by several hundred per cent.   The young fellow had
the air of a self-confident rustic, with little experience in the world.   Indeed, it seemed
from his elated manner as if this might be his
first trip from home, and the blowing of oil
wells an incidental speculation.   The Boy,

quick at inventive nomenclature, and fresh
from a reading of Robert Louis Stevenson,
called our visitor ''the Dynamiter,'' and by
that title I suppose we shall always remember him.

The Dynamiter confided to his listeners that
he was going down the river for ''a clean
hundred miles, and that's right smart fur, ain't
it? How fur down be yees goin'?'' The Doctor replied that we were going nine hundred;
whereat the man of explosives gave vent to
his feelings in a prolonged whistle, then a horse
laugh, and ''Oh come, now! Don' be givin'
us taffy! Say, hones' Injun, how fur down air
yew fellers goin', anyhow?'' It was with some
difficulty that he could comprehend the fact. A
hundred miles on the river was a great outing
for this village lad; nine hundred was rather
beyond his comprehension, although he finally
compromised by ''allowing'' that we might
be going as far as Cincinnati. Wouldn't the
Doctor go into partnership with him? He had
no caps for his cartridges, and if the Doctor
would buy caps and ''stan' in with him on the
cost of the glyser*een*,'' they would, regardless
of Ohio statutes, blow up the fish in unfre-
quented portions of the river, and make two

3

hundred dollars apiece by carrying the spoils
in to Wheeling.   The Doctor, as a law-abiding
citizen, good-naturedly declined; and upon my
return to the flat, the Dynamiter was handing
the Boy a huge stick of barber-pole candy,
saying, ''Well, yew fellers, we'll part friends,
anyhow—but sorry yew won't go in on this
spec'; there's right smart money in 't, 'n' don'
yer fergit it!''

By the middle of the afternoon we reached
the boundary line (40 miles) between Pennsylvania on the east and Ohio and West Virginia
on the west.   The last Pennsylvania settlements are a half mile above the boundary—
Smith's Ferry (right), an old and somewhat
decayed village, on a broad, low bottom at the
mouth of the picturesque Little Beaver Creek;*
and Georgetown (left), a prosperous-looking,
sedate town, with tidy lawns running down to
the edge of the terrace, below which is a shelving stone beach of generous width.   Two high
iron towers supporting the cable of a current
ferry add dignity to the twin settlements.   A

* On this creek was the hunting-cabin of the Seneca
(Mingo) chief, Half King, who sent a message of welcome to
Washington, when the latter was on his way to Great Mead-
ows (1754).

stone monument, six feet high, just observable
through the willows on the right shore, marks
the boundary; while upon the left bank, surmounting a high, rock-strewn beach, is the
dilapidated frame house of a West Virginia
"cracker," through whose garden-patch the
line takes its way, unobserved and unthought
of by pigs, chickens and children, which in
hopeless promiscuity swarm the interstate
premises.

For many days to come we are to have
Ohio on the right bank and West Virginia on
the left. There is no perceptible change, of
course, in the contour of the rugged hills which
hem us in; yet somehow it stirs the blood to
reflect that quite within the recollection of all
of us in Pilgrim's crew, save the Boy, that left
bank was the house of bondage, and that right
the land of freedom, and this river of ours the
highway between.

East Liverpool (44 miles) and Wellsville
(48 miles) are long stretches of pottery and
tile-making works, both of them on the Ohio
shore. There is nothing there to lure us, however, and we determined to camp on the banks
of Yellow Creek (51 miles), a peaceful little
Ohio stream some two rods in width, its mouth

crossed by two great iron spans, for railway
and highway. But although Yellow Creek
winds most gracefully and is altogether a
charming bit of rustic water, deep-set amid
picturesque slopes of field and wood, we fail
to find upon its banks an appropriate camping-
place. Upon one side a country road closely
skirts the shore, and on the other a railway,
while for the mile or more we pushed along
small farmsteads almost abutted. Hence we
retrace our path to the great river, and, dropping down-stream for two miles, find what we
seek upon the lower end of the chief of Kneistly's Cluster—two islands on the West Virginia
side of the channel.

It is storied ground, this neighborhood of
ours. Over there at the mouth of Yellow
Creek was, a hundred and twenty years ago,
the camp of Logan, the Mingo chief; opposite,
on the West Virginia shore, Baker's Bottom,
where occurred the treacherous massacre of
Logan's family. The tragedy is interwoven
with the history of the trans-Alleghany border;
and schoolboys have in many lands and tongues
recited the pathetic defense of the poor Mingo,
who, more sinned against than sinning, was
crushed in the inevitable struggle between

savagery and civilization. ''Who is there to mourn for Logan?"

We are high and dry on our willowed island. Above, just out of sight, are moored a brace of steam pile-drivers engaged in strengthening the dam which unites us with Baker's Bottom. To the left lies a broad stretch of gravel strand, beyond which is the narrow water fed by the overflow of the dam; to the right, the broad steamboat channel rolls between us and the Ohio hills, while the far-reaching vista down-stream is a feast of shade and tint, by land and water, with the lights and smoke of New Cumberland and Sloan's Station faintly discernible near the horizon. All about us lies a beautiful world of woodland. The whistle of quails innumerable broke upon us in the twilight, succeeding to the calls of rose-breasted grosbeaks and a goodly company of daylight followers; in this darkening hour, the low, plaintive note of the whip-poor-will is heard on every hand, now and then interrupted by the hoarse bark of owls. There is a gentle tinkling of cow-bells on the Ohio shore, and on both are human voices confused by distance. All pervading is the deep, sullen roar of a great wing-dam, a half mile or so down-stream.

The camp is gypsy-like. Our washing lies
spread on bushes, where it will catch the first
peep of morning sun. Perishable provisions
rest in notches of trees, where the cool evening
breeze will strike them. Seated upon the
"grub" box, I am writing up our log by aid of
the lantern hung from a branch overhead,
while W——, ever busy, sits by with her mending. Lying in the moonlight, which through
the sprawling willows gayly checkers our sand
bank, the Doctor and the Boy are discussing
the doings of Br'er Rabbit—for we are in the
Southland now, and may any day meet good
Uncle Remus.

CHAPTER IV.

An industrial region—Steubenville—Mingo Bottom — In a steel mill — Indian character.

Mingo Junction, Ohio, Wednesday, May 9th.—We had a cold night upon our island. Upon arising this morning, a heavy fog enveloped us, at first completely veiling the sun; soon it became faintly visible, a great ball of burnished copper reflected in the dimpled flood which poured between us and the Ohio shore. Weeds and willows were sopping wet, as was also our wash, and the breakfast fire was a comfortable companion. But by the time we were off, the cloud had lifted, and the sun gushed out with promise of a warm day.

Throughout the morning, Pilgrim glided through a thickly settled district, reminding us of the Monongahela. Sewer-pipe and vitrified-brick works, and iron and steel plants, abound on the narrow bottoms. The factories and mills themselves generally wear a pros-

39

perous look; but the dependent towns vary in
appearance, from clusters of shabby, down-at-
the-heel cabins, to lines of neat and well-
painted houses and shops.

We visited the vitrified-brick works at New
Cumberland, W. Va. (56 miles), where the
proprietor kindly explained his methods, and
talked freely of his business.   It was the old
story, too close a competition for profit,
although the use of brick pavements is fast
spreading.   Fire clay available for the purpose
is abundant on the banks of the Ohio all the
way from Pittsburg to Kingston (60 miles).
A few miles below New Cumberland, on the
Ohio shore, we inspected the tile works at
Freeman, and admired the dexterity which the
workmen had attained.

But what interested us most of all was the
appalling havoc which these clay and iron industries are making with the once beautiful
banks of the river.   Each of them has a large
daily output of debris, which is dumped unmercifully upon the water's edge in heaps from
fifty to a hundred feet high.   Sometimes for
nearly a mile in length, the natural bank is
deep buried out of sight; and we have from
our canoe naught but a dismal wall of rubbish,

crowding upon the river to the uttermost limit of governmental allowance. Fifty years hence, if these enterprises multiply at the present ratio, and continue their present methods, the Upper Ohio will roll between continuous banks of clay and iron offal, down to Wheeling and beyond.

Before noon we had left behind us this industrial region, and were again in rustic surroundings. The wind had gone down, the atmosphere was oppressively warm, the sun's reflection from the glassy stream came with almost scalding effect upon our faces. We had rigged an awning over some willow hoops, but it could not protect us from this reflection. For an hour or two—one may as well be honest—we fairly sweltered upon our pilgrimage, until at last a light breeze ruffled the water and brought blessed relief.

The hills are not as high as hitherto, and are more broken. Yet they have a certain majestic sweep, and for the most part are forest-mantled from base to summit. Between them the river winds with noble grace, continually giving us fresh vistas, often of surpassing loveliness. The bottoms are broader now, and frequently semicircular, with fine farms upon them, and prosperous villages nestled in generous groves. Many of the houses betoken age, or what passes for it in this relatively new country, being of the colonial pattern, with fan-shaped windows above the doors, Grecian pillars flanking the front porch, and wearing the air of comfortable respectability.

Beautiful islands lend variety to the scene, some of them mere willowed "tow-heads" largely submerged in times of flood, while others are of a permanent character, often occupied by farms. We have with us a copy of Cuming's *Western Pilot* (Cincinnati, 1834), which is still a practicable guide for the Ohio, as the river's shore lines are not subject to so rapid changes as those of the Mississippi; but many of the islands in Cuming's are not now to be found, having been swept away in floods, and we encounter few new ones. It is clear that the islands are not so numerous as sixty years ago. The present works of the United States Corps of Engineers tend to permanency in the *status quo;* doubtless the government map of 1881 will remain an authoritative chart for a half century or more to come.

W—'s enthusiasm for botany frequently takes us ashore. Landing at the foot of some

eroded steep which, with ragged charm, rises
sharply from the gravelly beach, we fasten
Pilgrim's painter to a stone, and go scrambling
over the hillside in search of flowers, bearing
in mind the Boy's constant plea, to "Get only
one of a kind," and leave the rest for seed;
for other travelers may come this way, and
'tis a sin indeed to exterminate a botanical
rarity. But we find no rarities to-day—only
solomon's seal, trillium, wild ginger, cranebill,
jack-in-the-pulpit, wild columbine. Poison
ivy is on every hand, in these tangled woods,
with ferns of many varieties—chiefly maiden-
hair, walking leaf, and bladder. The view
from projecting rocks, in these lofty places, is
ever inspiring; the country spread out below
us, as in a relief map; the great glistening
river winding through its hilly trough; a
rumpled country for a few miles on either side,
gradually trending into broad plains, checkered
with fields on which farmsteads and rustic
villages are the chessmen.

At one o'clock we were at Steubenville,
Ohio (67 miles), where the broad stoned wharf
leads sharply up to the smart, well-built, substantial town of some sixteen thousand inhabitants. W— and I had some shopping to do

there, while the Doctor and the Boy remained down at the inevitable wharf-boat, and gossiped with the philosophical agent, who bemoaned the decadence of steamboat traffic in general, and the rapidly falling stage of water in particular.

Three miles below Steubenville is Mingo Junction, where we are the guests of a friend who is superintendent of the iron and steel works here. The population of Mingo is twenty-five hundred. From seven to twelve hundred are employed in the works, according to the exigencies of business. Ten per cent of them are Hungarians and Slavonians—a larger proportion would be dangerous, our host avers, because of the tendency of these people to "run the town" when sufficiently numerous to make it possible. The Slavs in the iron towns come to America for a few years, intent solely on saving every dollar within reach. They are willing to work for wages which from the American standard seem low, but to them almost fabulous; herd together in surprising promiscuity; maintain a low scale of clothing and diet, often to the ruin of health; and eventually return to Eastern Europe, where their savings constitute a little fortune upon

which they can end their days in ease. This
sort of competition is fast degrading legitimate
American labor. Its regulation ought not to
be thought impossible.

A visit to a great steel-making plant, in full
operation, is an event in a man's life. Particularly remarkable is the weird spectacle
presented at night, with the furnaces fiercely
gleaming, the fresh ingots smoking hot, the
Bessemer converter "blowing off," the great
cranes moving about like things of life, bearing
giant kettles of molten steel; and amidst it
all, human life held so cheaply. Nearer to
mediæval notions of hell comes this fiery scene
than anything imagined by Dante. The working life of one of these men is not over ten
years, B— says. A decade of this intense
heat, compared to which a breath of outdoor
air in the close mill-yard, with the midsummer
sun in the nineties, seems chilly, wears a man
out—"only fit for the boneyard then, sir,"
was the laconic estimate of an intelligent boss
whom I questioned on the subject.

Wages run from ninety cents to five dollars
a day, with far more at the former rate than
the latter. A ninety-cent man working in a
place so hot that were water from a hose turned

upon him it would at once be resolved into scalding steam, deserves our sympathy. It is pleasing to find in our friend, the superintendent, a strong fellow-feeling for his men, and a desire to do all in his power to alleviate their condition. He has accomplished much in improving the *morale* of the town; but deep-seated, inexorable economic conditions, apparently beyond present control, render nugatory any attempts to better the financial condition of the underpaid majority.

Mingo Junction—"Mingo Bottom" of old—was an interesting locality in frontier days. On this fertile river beach was long one of the strongest of the Mingo villages. During the last week of May, 1782, Crawford's little army rendezvoused here, en route to Sandusky, a hundred and fifty miles distant, and intent on the destruction of the Wyandot towns. But the Indians had not been surprised, and the army was driven back with slaughter, reaching Mingo the middle of June, bereft of its commander. Crawford, who was a warm friend of Washington, suffered almost unprecedented torture at the stake, his fate sending a thrill of horror through all the Western settlements.

Let us not be too harsh in our judgment of

these red Indians.   At first, the white colonists from Europe were regarded by them as
of supernatural origin, and hospitality, vener-
ation, and confidence were displayed toward
the new-comers.   But the mortality of the
Europeans was soon made painfully evident
to them.   When the early Spaniards, and
afterward the English, kidnaped tribesmen
for sale into slavery, or for use as captive
guides, and even murdered them on slight
provocation, distrust and hatred naturally succeeded to the sentiment of awe.   Like many
savage races, like the earlier Romans, the Indian looked upon the member of every tribe
with which he had not made a formal peace
as a public enemy; hence he felt justified in
wreaking his vengeance on the race, whenever
he failed to find individual offenders.   He was
exceptionally cruel, his mode of warfare was
skulking, he could not easily be reached in the
forest fastnesses which he alone knew well,
and his strokes fell heaviest on women and
children; so that whites came to fear and un-
speakably to loathe the savage, and often
added greatly to the bitterness of the struggle
by retaliation in kind.   The white borderers
themselves were frequently brutal, reckless,

lawless; and under such conditions, clashing was inevitable. But worse agents of discord than the agricultural colonists were the itinerants who traveled through the woods visiting the tribes, exchanging goods for furs; these often cheated and robbed the Indian, taught him the use of intoxicants, bullied and browbeat him, appropriated his women, and in general introduced serious demoralization into the native camps. The bulk of the whites doubtless intended to treat the Indian honorably; but the forest traders were beyond the pale of law, and news of the details of their transactions seldom reached the coast settlements.

As a neighbor, the Indian was difficult to deal with, whether in the negotiation of treaties of amity, or in the purchase of lands. Having but a loose system of government, there was no really responsible head, and no compact was secure from the interference of malcontents, who would not be bound by treaties made by the chiefs. The English felt that the red men were not putting the land to its full use, that much of the territory was growing up as a waste, that they were best entitled to it who could make it the most productive. On

the other hand, the earlier cessions of land
were made under a total misconception; the
Indians supposed that the new-comers would,
after a few years of occupancy, pass on and
leave the tract again to the natives.   There
was no compromise possible between races
with precisely opposite views of property in
land.   The struggle was inevitable—civilization against savagery.   No sentimental notions
could prevent it.   It was in the nature of
things that the weaker must give way.   The
Indian was a formidable antagonist, and there
were times when the result of the struggle
seemed uncertain; but in the end he went to
the wall.   In judging the vanquished enemy
of our civilization, let us not underestimate his
intellect, or the many good qualities which
were mingled with his savage vices, or fail to
credit him with sublime courage, and a tribal
patriotism which no disaster could cool.

4

CHAPTER V.

HOUSEBOAT LIFE — DECADENCE OF STEAM-
BOAT TRAFFIC—WHEELING, AND WHEELING
CREEK.

ABOVE MOUNDSVILLE, W. VA., Thursday,
May 10th.—Our friends saw us off at the
gravelly beach just below the "works." There
was a slight breeze ahead, but the atmosphere
was agreeable, and Pilgrim bore a happy crew,
now as brown as gypsies; the first painful effects
of sunburn are over, and we are hardened in
skin and muscle to any vicissitudes which are
likely to be met upon our voyage. Rough
weather, river mud, and all the other exigencies
of a moving camp, are beginning to tell upon
clothing; we are becoming like gypsies in raiment, as well as color. But what a soul-
satisfying life is this gypsying! We possess
the world, while afloat on the Ohio!

There are, in the course of the summer, so
many sorts of people traveling by the river,—
steamboat passengers, campers, fishers, house-

boat folk, and what not,—that we attract little
attention of ourselves, but Pilgrim is indeed a
curiosity hereabout.   What remarks we over-
hear are about her,—"Honey skiff, that!"
"Right smart skiff!"   "Good skiff for her
place, but no good for this yere river!" and
so on.   She is a lap-streak, square-sterned
craft, of white cedar three-eighths of an inch
thick; fifteen feet in length and four of beam;
weighs just a hundred pounds; comfortably
holds us and our luggage, with plenty of
spare room to move about in; is easily pro-
pelled, and as stanch as can be made.   Upon
these waters, we meet nothing like her.   Not
counting the curious floating boxes and
punts, which are knocked together out of
driftwood, by boys and poor whites, and are
numerous all along shore, the regulation
Ohio river skiff is built on graceful lines,
but of inch boards, heavily ribbed, and is a
sorry weight to handle.   The contention is,
that to withstand the swash of steamboat
wakes breaking upon the shore, and the rush
of drift in times of flood, a heavy skiff is necessary; there is a tendency to decry Pilgrim
as a plaything, unadapted to the great river.
A reasonable degree of care at all times, how-

ever, and keeping the boat drawn high on the
beach when not in use,—such care as we
are familiar with upon our Wisconsin inland
lakes,—would render the employment of such
as she quite practicable, and greatly lessen the
labor of rowing on this waterway.

The houseboats, dozens of which we see
daily, interest us greatly. They are scows, or
"flats," greatly differing in size, with low-
ceilinged cabins built upon them—sometimes
of one room, sometimes of half a dozen, and
varying in character from a mere shanty to a
well-appointed cottage. Perhaps the greater
number of these craft are afloat in the river,
and moored to the bank, with a gang-plank
running to shore; others are "beached," having found a comfortable nook in some higher
stage of water, and been fastened there,
propped level with timbers and driftwood.
Among the houseboat folk are young working
couples starting out in life, and hoping ulti-
mately to gain a foothold on land; unfortunate
people, who are making a fresh start; men
regularly employed in riverside factories and
mills; invalids, who, at small expense, are
trying the fresh-air cure; others, who drift up
and down the Ohio, seeking casual work; and

legitimate fishermen, who find it convenient to be near their nets, and to move about according to the needs of their calling. But a goodly proportion of these boats are inhabited by the lowest class of the population,—poor "crackers" who have managed to scrape together enough money to buy, or enough energy and driftwood to build, such a craft; and, near or at the towns, many are occupied by gamblers, illicit liquor dealers, and others who, while plying nefarious trades, make a pretense of following the occupation of the Apostles.

Houseboat people, whether beached or afloat, pay no rent, and heretofore have paid no taxes. Kentucky has recently passed, more as a police regulation than as a means of revenue, an act levying a State tax of twenty-five dollars upon each craft of this character; and the other commonwealths abutting upon the river are considering the policy of doing likewise. The houseboat men have, however, recently formed a protective association, and propose to fight the new laws on constitutional grounds, the contention being that the Ohio is a national highway, and that commerce upon it cannot be hampered by State taxes. This view does not, however, affect the taxability of "beached" boats, which are clearly squatters on State soil.

Both in town and country, the riffraff of the houseboat element are in disfavor. It is not uncommon for them, beached or tied up, to remain unmolested in one spot for years, with their pigs, chickens, and little garden patch about them, mayhap a swarm or two of bees, and a cow enjoying free pasturage along the weedy bank or on neighboring hills. Occasionally, however, as the result of spasmodic local agitation, they are by wholesale ordered to betake themselves to some more hospitable shore; and not a few farmers, like our friend at Beaver River, are quick to pattern after the city police, and order their visitors to move on the moment they seek a mooring. For the truth is, the majority of those who ''live on the river,'' as the phrase goes, have the reputation of being pilferers; farmers tell sad tales of despoiled chicken-roosts and vegetable gardens. From fishing, shooting, collecting chance driftwood, and leading a desultory life along shore, like the wreckers of old they naturally fall into this thieving habit. Having neither rent nor taxes to pay, and for the most part not voting, and having no share in the polit-

ical or social life of landsmen, they are in the
State, yet not of it,—a class unto themselves,
whose condition is well worthy the study of
economists.

Interspersed with the houseboat folk, although of diffcrent character, are those whose
business leads them to dwell as nomads upon
the river—merchant peddlers, who spend a
day or two at some rustic landing, while scour-
ing the neighborhood for oil-barrels and junk,
which they load in great heaps upon the flat
roofs of their cabins, giving therefor, at goodly
prices, groceries, crockery, and notions,—
often bartering their wares for eggs and dairy
products, to be disposed of to passing steamers, whose clerks in turn "pack" them for the
largest market on their route; blacksmiths,
who moor their floating shops to country beach
or village levee, wherever business can be had;
floating theaters and opera companies, with
large barges built as play-houses, towed from
town to town by their gaudily-painted tugs, on
which may occasionally be perched the vociferous "steam piano" of our circus days,
"whose soul-stirring music can be heard for
four miles;" traveling sawyers, with old steamboats made over into sawmills, employed by

farmers to "work up" into lumber such logs
as they can from time to time bring down to
the shore—the product being oftenest used in
the neighborhood, but occasionally rafted, and
floated to the nearest large town; and a miscellaneous lot of traveling craftsmen who live
and work afloat,—chairmakers, upholsterers,
feather and mattress renovators, photogra-
phers,—who land at the villages, scatter abroad
their advertising cards, and stay so long as the
ensuing patronage warrants.

A motley assortment, these neighbors of ours,
an uncultivated field for the fiction writers.
We have struck up acquaintance with many
of them, and they are not bad fellows, as the
world goes. Philosophers all, and loquacious
to a degree. But they cannot, for the life of
them, fathom the mystery of our cruise. We
are not in trade? we are not fishing? we
are not canvassers? we are not show-people?
"What 'n 'tarnation air ye, anny way? Oh,
come now! No fellers is do'n' th' river fur
fun, that's sartin—ye're jist gov'm'nt agints!
Thet's my way o' think'n'. Well, 'f ye kin
find fun in 't, then done go ahead, I say! But
all same, we'll be friends, won't we? Yew bet,
strangers! Ye're welcome t' all in this yere

shanty boat—ain't no bakky 'bout yer close, yew fellers?" We meet with abundant courtesy of this rude sort, and weaponless sleep well o' nights, fearing naught from our comrades for the nonce.

We again have railways on either bank. The iron horse has almost eclipsed the "fire canoe," as the Indians picturesquely styled the steamboat. We occasionally see boats tied up to the wharves, evidently not in commission; but, in actual operation, we seldom meet or pass over one or two daily. To be sure, the low stage of water,—from six to eight feet thus far, and falling daily,—and the coal strike, militate against navigation interests. But the truth is, there is very little business now left for steamboats, beyond the movement of coal, stone, bricks, and other bulky material, some way freight, and a light passenger traffic. The railroads are quicker and surer, and of course competition lowers the charges.

The heavy manufacturing interests along the river now depend little upon the steamers, although originally established here because of them. I asked our friend, the superintendent at Mingo, what advantage was gained by having his plant upon the river. He replied:

"We can get all the water we want, and we use a great deal of it; and it is convenient to empty our slag upon the banks; but our chief interest here is in the fact that Mingo is a railway junction." By rail he gets his coal and ore, and ships away his product. Were the coal to come a considerable distance, the river would be the cheaper road; but it is obtained from neighboring hill mines that are practically owned by the railways. This coal, by the way, costs $1.10 at the shaft mouth, and $1.75 landed at the Mingo works. As for the sewer-pipe, brick, and pottery works, they are along stream because of the great beds of clay exposed by the erosion of the river.

It is fortunate for the stability of these towns, that the Ohio flows along the trans-continental pathway westward, so that the great railway lines may serve them without deflection from their natural course. Had the great stream flowed south instead of west, the industries of the valley doubtless would gradually have been removed to the transverse highways of the new commerce, save where these latter crossed the river, and thus have left scores of once thriving communities mere 'longshore wrecks of their former selves. This is not possible, now. The steamboat traffic may still further waste, until the river is no longer serviceable save as a continental drainage ditch; but, chiefly because of its railways, the Ohio Valley will continue to be the seat of an industrial population which shall wax fat upon the growth of the nation's needs.

By the middle of the afternoon, we were at Wheeling (91 miles). The town has fifty thousand inhabitants, is substantially built, of a distinctly Southern aspect; well stretched out along the river, but narrow; with gaunt, treeless, gully-washed hills of clay rising abruptly behind, giving the place a most forbidding appearance from the water. There are several fine bridges spanning the Ohio; and Wheeling Creek, which empties on the lower edge of town, is crossed by a maze of steel spans and stone arches; the well-paved wharf, sloping upward from the Ohio, is nearly as broad and imposing as that of Pittsburg;* houseboats are here by the score, some of them

* Upon the Ohio and kindred rivers, the term "wharf" applies to the river beach when graded and paved, ready for the reception of steamers. Such a wharf must not be confounded with a lake or seaside wharf, a staging projected into the water.

the haunts of fishing clubs, as we judge from the names emblazoned on their sides—"Mystic Crew," "South Side Club," and the like.

For the first time upon our tour, negroes are abundant upon the streets and lounging along the river front. They vary in color from yellow to inky blackness, and in raiment from the "dude," smart in straw hat, collars and cuffs, and white-frilled shirt with glass-diamond pin, to the steamboat roustabout, all slouch and rags, and evil-eyed.

Wheeling Island (300 acres), up to thirty years ago mentioned in travelers' journals as a rare beauty-spot, is to-day thick-set with cottages of factory hands and small villas, and commonplace; while smoky Bridgeport, opposite on the Ohio side, was from our vantage-point a mere smudge upon the landscape.

Wheeling Creek is famous in Western history. The three Zane brothers, Ebenezer, Jonathan and Silas,—typical, old-fashioned names these, bespeaking the God-fearing, Bible-loving, Scotch-Presbyterian stock from which sprang so large a proportion of trans-Alleghany pioneers,—explored this region as early as 1769, built cabins, and made improvements—Silas at the forks of the creek, and

Ebenezer and Jonathan at the mouth. During three or four years, it was a hard fight between them and the Indians; but, though several times driven from the scene, the Zane brothers stubbornly reappeared, and rebuilt their burned habitations.

Before the Revolutionary War broke out, the fortified home of the Zanes, at the creek mouth, was a favorite stopping stage in the savage-haunted wilderness; and many a traveler in those early days has left us in his journal a thankful account of his tarrying here. The Zane stockade developed into Fort Fincastle, in Lord Dunmore's time; then, Fort Henry, during the Revolution; and everyone who knows his Western history at all has read of the three famous sieges of Wheeling (1777, 1781, and 1782), and the daring deeds of its men and women, which help illumine the pages of border annals. Finally, by 1784, the fort at Wheeling, that had never surrendered, was demolished as no longer necessary, for the wall of savage resistance was now pushed far westward. Wheeling had become the western end of a wagon road across the Panhandle, from Redstone, and here were fitted out many flatboat expeditions for the lower Ohio; later,

in steamboat· days, the shallow water of the
upper river caused Wheeling to be in midsummer the highest port attainable; and to this
day it holds its ground as the upper terminus
of several steamboat lines.

Below Wheeling are several miles of factory
towns nestled by the strand, and numerous
coal tipples, with their begrimed villages.
Fishermen have been frequent to-day, in
houseboats of high and low degree, and in
land camps composed of tents and board shanties, with rows of seines and tarred pound-nets
stretched in the sun to dry; tow-headed children abound, almost as nude as the pigs and
dogs and chickens amongst which they waddle
and roll; women-folk busy themselves with
the multifarious cares of home-keeping, while
their lords are in shady nooks mending nets,
or listlessly examining trout lines which appear to yield but empty hooks; they tell us
that when the river is falling, fish bite not, and
yet they serenely angle on, dreaming their
lives away.

A half mile above Big Grave Creek (101
miles), we, too, hurry into camp on a shelving
bank of sand, deep-fringed with willows; for
over the western hills thunder-clouds are rising,

with wind gusts. Level fields stretch back of us for a quarter of a mile, to the hills which bound the bottom; at our front door majestically rolls the growing river, perhaps a third of a mile in width, black with the reflection of the sky, and wrinkled now and then with squalls which scurry over its bubbling surface. *

The storm does not break, but the bending tree-tops crone, and toads innumerable rend the air with their screaming whistles. We had great ado, during the cooking of dinner, to prevent them from hopping into our little stove, as it gleamed brightly in the early dusk; and have adopted special precautions to keep them from the tent, as they jump about in the tall grass, appeasing their insectivorous appetites.

---

* It was in this neighborhood, a mile or two above our camp, where the bottom is narrower, that Capt. William Foreman and twenty other Virginia militiamen were killed in an Indian ambuscade, Sept. 27, 1777. An inscribed stone monument was erected on the spot in 1835, but we could not find it.

CHAPTER VI.

THE BIG GRAVE—WASHINGTON, AND ROUND
BOTTOM—A LAZY MAN'S PARADISE—CAP-
TINA CREEK—GEORGE ROGERS CLARK AT
FISH CREEK—SOUTHERN TYPES.

NEAR FISHING CREEK, Friday, May 11th.
—There had been rain during the night, with
fierce wind gusts, but during breakfast the
atmosphere quieted, and we had a genial,
semi-cloudy morning.

Off at 8 o'clock, Pilgrim's crew were soon
exploring Moundsville. There are five thousand people in this old, faded, countrified
town. They show you with pride the State
Penitentiary of West Virginia, a solemn-look-
ing pile of dark gray stone, with the feeble
battlements and towers common to American
prison architecture. But the chief feature of
the place is the great Indian mound—the "Big
Grave" of early chroniclers. This earthwork
is one of the largest now remaining in the
United States, being sixty-eight feet high and

a hundred in diameter at the base, and has for over a century attracted the attention of travelers and archæologists.

We found it at the end of a straggling street, on the edge of the town, a quarter of a mile back from the river. Around the mound has been left a narrow plat of ground, utilized as a cornfield; and the stout picket fence which encloses it bears peremptory notice that admission is forbidden. However, as the proprietor was not easily accessible, we exercised the privilege of historical pilgrims, and, letting ourselves in through the gate, picked our way through rows of corn, and ascended the great cone. It is covered with a heavy growth of white oaks, some of them three feet in diameter, among which the path picturesquely zigzags. The summit is fifty-five feet in diameter, and the center somewhat depressed, like a basin. From the middle of this basin a shaft some twenty-five feet in diameter has been sunk by explorers, for a distance of perhaps fifty feet; at one time, a level tunnel connected the bottom of this shaft with the side of the cone, but it has been mostly obliterated. A score of years ago, tunnel and shaft were utilized as the leading attractions of a

5

beer garden—to such base uses may a great historical landmark descend!

Dickens, who apparently wrote the greater part of his *American Notes* while suffering from dyspepsia, has a note of appreciation for the Big Grave: ". . . the host of Indians who lie buried in a great mound yonder—so old that mighty oaks and other forest trees have struck their roots into its earth; and so high that it is a hill, even among the hills that Nature planted around it. The very river, as though it shared one's feelings of compassion for the extinct tribes who lived so pleasantly here, in their blessed ignorance of white existence, hundreds of years ago, steals out of its way to ripple near this mound; and there are few places where the Ohio sparkles more brightly than in the Big Grave Creek."

There is a sharp bend in the river, just below Moundsville, with Dillon's Bottom stretching long and wide at the apex on the Ohio shore—flat green fields, dotted with little white farmsteads, each set low in its apple grove, and a convoluted wall of dark hills hemming them in along the northern horizon. Then below this comes Round Bottom, its counterpart on the West Virginia side, and coursing through it a pretty meadow creek, Butler's Run.

Writes Washington, in 1781, to a correspondent who is thinking of renting lands in this region: " I have a small tract called the round bottom containing about 600 Acres, which would also let. It lyes on the Ohio, opposite to pipe Creek, and a little above Capteening." Across the half mile of river are the little levels and great slopes of the Ohio hills, through which breaks this same Pipe Creek; and hereabout Cresap's band murdered a number of inoffensive Shawanese, a tragedy which was one of the inciting causes of Lord Dunmore's War (1774).

We crossed over into Ohio, and pulled up on the gravelly spit at the mouth of Pipe. While the others were botanizing high on the mountain side, I went along a beach path toward a group of whitewashed cabins, intent on replenishing the canteen. Upon opening the gate of one of them, two grizzly dogs came bounding out, threatening to test the strength of my corduroy trousers. The proprietor cautiously peered from a window, and, much to my relief, called off the animals. Satisfied, apparently, that I was not the visitor he ex-

pected, the fellow lounged out and sat upon
the steps, where I joined him.   He was a tall,
raw-boned, loose-jointed young man, with a
dirty, buttonless flannel shirt which revealed
a hairy breast; upon his trousers hung a variety
of patches, in many stages of grease and decrepitude; a gray slouch hat shaded his little
fishy eyes and hollow, yellow cheeks; and the
snaky ends of his yellow mustache were stiff
with accumulations of dried tobacco juice.
His fat, waddling wife, in a greasy black gown,
followed with bare feet, and, arms akimbo,
listened in the open door.

A coal company owns the rocky river front,
here and at many places below, and lets these
cabins to the poor-white element, so numerous
on the Ohio's banks.   The renter is privileged
to cultivate whatever land he can clear on the
rocky, precipitous slopes, which is seldom
more than half an acre to the cabin; and he
may, if he can afford a cow, let her run wild
in the scrub.   The coal vein, a few rods back
of the house, is only a few inches thick, and
poor in quality, but is freely resorted to by the
cotters.   He worked whenever he could find
a job, my host said—in the coal mines and

quarries, or on the bottom farms, or the rail-
road which skirts the bank at his feet.

"But I tell ye, sir, th' *I*talians and Hungarians is spoil'n' this yere country fur white
men; 'n' I do'n' see no prospect for hits be'n'
better till they get shoved out uv 't!" Yet he
said that life wasn't so hard here as it was in
some parts he had heard tell of—the climate
was mild, that he "'lowed;" a fellow could go
out and get a free bucket of coal from the hillside "back yon;" he might get all the "light
wood 'n' patchin' stuff" he wanted, from the
river drift; could, when he "hankered after
'em," catch fish off his own front-door yard;
and pick up a dollar now and then at odd jobs,
when the rent was to be paid, or the "ol'
woman" wanted a dress, or he a new coat.

This is clearly the lazy man's Paradise. I
do not remember to have heard that the South
Sea Islanders, in the ante-missionary days,
had an easier time of it than this. What new
fortune will befall my friend when he gets the
Italians and Hungarians "shoved out," and
"things pick up a bit," I cannot conceive.

A pleasing panorama he has from his doorway—across the river, the fertile fields of
Round Bottom, once Washington's; Captina

Island, just below, long and thickly-willowed, dreamily afloat in a glassy sea, reflecting every change of light; the whole girt about with the wide uplands of the winding valley, and overhead the march of sunny clouds.

Captina Creek (108 miles) is not far down on the Ohio bank, and beside it the little hamlet of Powhattan Point, with the West Virginia hills thereabout exceptionally high and steep, and wooded to the very top. Washington, who knew the Ohio well, down to the Great Kanawha, wrote of this creek in 1770: "A pretty large creek on the west side, called by Nicholson [his interpreter] Fox-Grape-Vine, by others Captema creek, on which, eight miles up, is the town called Grape-Vine Town." Captina village is its white successor. But there were also Indians at the mouth of the creek; for when George Rogers Clark and his missionary companion, Jones, two years later camped opposite on the Virginia shore, they went over to make a morning call on the natives, who repaid it in the evening, doubtless each time receiving freely from the white men's bounty.

The next day was Sunday, and the travelers remained in camp, Jones recording in his **jour-**

nal that he "instructed what Indians came over." In the course of his prayer, the missionary was particularly impressed by the attitude of the chief of Grape-Vine Town, named Frank Stephens, who professed to believe in the Christian God; and he naively writes, "I was informed that, all the time, the Indians looked very seriously at me." Jones appears to have been impressed also with the hardness of the beach, where they camped in the open, doubtless to avoid surprises: "Instead of feathers, my bed was gravel-stones, by the river side . . . which at first seemed not to suit me, but afterward it became more natural."

In those days, traveling was beset with difficulties, both ashore and afloat. Eight years later (spring of 1780), three flatboats were descending the Ohio, laden with families intending to settle in Kentucky, when they suffered a common fate, being attacked by Indians off Captina Creek. Several men and a child were killed, and twenty-one persons were carried into captivity—among them, Catherine Malott, a girl in her teens, who subsequently became the wife of that most notorious of border renegades, Simon Girty.

On the West Virginia shore, not over a third of a mile below Captina Creek, empties Grave Yard Run, a modest rivulet. It would of itself not be noticeable amid the crowd of minor creeks and runs, coursing down to the great river through rugged ravines which corrugate the banks. But it has a history. Here, late in October or early in November, 1772, young George Rogers Clark made his first stake west of the Alleghanies, rudely cultivating a few acres of forest land on what is now called Cresap's Bottom, surveying for the neighbors, and in the evenings teaching their children in the little log cabin of his friend, Yates Conwell, at the mouth of Fish Creek, a few miles below. Fish Creek was in itself famous as one of the sections of the great Indian trail, "The Warrior Branch," which, starting in Tennessee, came northward through Kentucky and Southern Ohio, and, proceeding by way of this creek, crossed over to Dunkard Creek, thence to the mouth of Redstone. Washington stopped at Conwell's in March or April, 1774; but Clark was away from home at the time, and the "Father of his Country" never met the man who has been dubbed the "Washington of the West." Lord Dunmore's War was hatching, and a few months later the Fish Creek surveyor and schoolmaster had entered upon his life work as an Indian fighter.

At Bearsville (126 miles) we first meet a phenomenon common to the Ohio—the edges of the alluvial bottom being higher than the fields back of them, forming a natural levee, above which curiously rise to our view the spires and chimneys of the village. Harris' *Journal* (1803) made early note of this, and advanced an acceptable theory: "We frequently remarked that the banks are higher at the margin than at a little distance back. I account for it in this manner: Large trees, which are brought down the river by the inundations, are lodged upon the borders of the bank, but cannot be floated far upon the champaign, because obstructed by the growth of wood. Retaining their situation when the waters subside, they obstruct and detain the leaves and mud, which would else recoil into the stream, and thus, in process of time, form a bank higher than the interior flats."

Tied up to Bearsville landing is a gayly painted barge, the home of Price's Floating Opera Company, and in front its towing-steamer, "Troubadour." A steam calliope is

part of the visible furniture of the establishment, and its praises as a noise-maker are
sung in large type in the handbills which, with
numerous colored lithographs of the perform-
ers, adorn the shop windows in the neighboring
river towns.

Two miles farther down, on a high bank at
the mouth of Fishing Creek, lies New Martinsville, West Va. (127 miles), a rather shabby
town of fifteen hundred souls. As W— and
I passed up the main street, seeking for a
grocery, we noticed that the public hall was
being decorated for a dance to come off to-
night; and placards advertising the event were
everywhere rivaling the gaudy prints of the
floating opera.

Meanwhile, a talkative native was inter-
viewing the Doctor, down at the river side.
It required some good-natured fencing on the
part of our skipper to prevent the Virginian
from learning all about our respective families
away back to the third generation. He was
a short, chubby man, with a Dixie goatee, his
flannel shirt negligée, and a wide-brimmed
straw hat jauntily set on the back of his head.
He was sociable, and sat astride of our beached
prow, punctuating his remarks with squirts of

tobacco juice, and a bit of lath with which he meditatively tapped the gunwale, the meantime, with some skill, casting pebbles into the water with his bare toes. "Ax'n yer pardon, ma'm!" he said, scrambling from his perch upon W —'s appearance; and then, pushing us off, he bowed with much Southern gallantry, and hat in hand begged we would come again to New Martinsville, and stay longer.

The hills lining these reaches are lower than above, yet graceful in their sweeping lines. Conical mounds sometimes surmount them, relics of the prehistoric time when our Indians held to the curious fashion of building earthworks. We no longer entertain the notion that a separate and a prouder race of wild men than we know erected these tumuli. That pleasant fiction has departed from us; but the works are none the less interesting, now that more is known of their origin.

Two miles below New Martinsville, on the West Virginia shore, we pitch camp, just as the light begins to sink over the Ohio hills. The atmosphere is sweet with the odor of wild grape blossoms, and the willow also is in bloom. Poison ivy, to whose baneful touch fortunately none of us appear susceptible, grows

everywhere about.   From the farmhouse on
the narrow bottom to our rear comes the me-
lodious tinkle-tinkle of cow bells.   The operatic calliope is in full blast, at Bearsville, its
shrieks and snorts coming down to us through
four miles of space, all too plainly borne by
the northern breeze; and now and then we
hear the squeak of the New Martinsville fiddles.
There are no mosquitoes as yet, but burly May-
chafers come stupidly dashing against our tent,
and the toads are piping merrily.

CHAPTER VII.

ABOVE MARIETTA, Saturday, May 12th.—
Since the middle of yesterday afternoon we
have been in Dixie,—that is, when we are on
the West Virginia shore.   The famous Mason
and Dixon Line (lat. 39° 43′ 26″) touches the
Ohio at the mouth of Proctor's Run (121½
miles).

There was a heavy fog this morning, on
land and river.   But through shifting rifts
made by the morning breeze, we had kaleidoscopic, cloud-framed pictures of the dark, jut-
ting headlands which hem us in; of little white
cabins clustered by the country road which on
either bank crawls along narrow terraces between overtopping steeps and sprawling beach,
or winds through fertile bottoms, according to
whether the river approaches or recedes from
its inclosing bluffs; of hillside fields, tipped at

77

various angles of ascent, sometimes green with
springing grain, but oftenest gray or brown or
yellow, freshly planted,—charming patches of
color, in this somber-hued world of sloping
woodland.

At Williamson's Island (134 miles) the fog
lifted.   The air was heavy with the odor of
petroleum.   All about us were the ugly, towering derricks of oil and natural gas wells—
Witten's Bottom on the right, with its abutting
hills; the West Virginia woods across the river,
and the maple-strewn island between, all covered with scaffolds.   The country looks like a
rumpled fox-and-geese board, with pegs stuck
all over it.   A mile and a half below lies Sis-
tersville, W. Va., the emporium of this greasy
neighborhood—great red oil-tanks and smoky
refineries its chiefest glory; crude and raw, like
the product it handles.   We landed at Witten's Bottom,—W—, the Boy, and I,—while
the Doctor, philosophically preferring to take
the oily elephant for granted, piloted Pilgrim
to the rendezvous a mile below.

Oil was ''struck'' here two or three years
ago, and now within a distance of a few miles
there are hundreds of wells—''two hun'rd in
this yere gravel alone, sir!''   I was told by a

red-headed man in a red shirt, who lived with
his numerous family in a twelve-foot-square
box at the rear of a pumping engine. An engine serves several wells,—the tumbling-rods,
rudely boxed in, stretching off through the
fields and over the hills to wherever needed.
The operatives dwell in little shanties scattered
conveniently about; in front of each is a vertical half-inch pipe, six or eight feet high,
bearing a half bushel of natural-gas flame
which burns and tosses night and day, winter
and summer, making the Bottom a warm corner of the earth, when the unassisted temperature is in the eighties. It is a bewildering
scene, with all these derricks thickly scattered
around, engines noisily puffing, walking-beams
forever rearing and plunging, the country cob-
webbed with tumbling-rods and pipe lines, the
shanties of the operatives with their rude lamp-
posts, and the face of Nature so besmeared
with the crude output of the wells that every
twig and leaf is thick with grease.

Just above Witten's commences the Long
Reach of the Ohio—a charming panorama, for
sixteen and a half miles in a nearly straight
line to the southwest. Little towns line the
alternating bottoms, and farmsteads are nu-

merous on the slopes. But they are rocky and narrow, these gentle shoulders of the hills, and a poor class of folk occupy them—half fishers, half farmers, a cross between my Round Bottom friend and the houseboat nomads.

A picturesquely-dilapidated log house, with whitewashed porch in front, and a vine arbor at the rear, attracted our attention at the foot of the reach, near Grape Island. I clambered up, to photograph it. The ice was broken by asking for a drink of water. A gaunt girl of eighteen, the elder of two, with bare feet, her snaky hair streaming unkempt about a smirking face, went with a broken-nosed pitcher to a run, which could be heard splashing over its rocky bed near by. The meanwhile, I took a seat in the customary arcade between the living room and kitchen, and talked with her fat, greasy, red-nosed father, who confided to me that he was "a pi'neer from way back." He occupied his own land—a rare circumstance among these riverside "crackers;" had a hundred and thirty acres, worth twenty dollars the acre; "jist yon ways," back of the house, in the cliff-side, there was a coal vein two feet thick, as yet only "worked" for his own fuel; and lately, he had struck a bank of firebrick clay which might some day be a "good thing for th' gals."

On leaving, I casually mentioned my desire to photograph the family on the porch, where the light was good. While I walked around the house outside, they passed through the front room, which seemed to be the common dormitory as well as parlor. To my surprise and chagrin, the girls and their dowdy mother had, in those brief moments of transition, contrived to arrange their hair and dress to a degree which took from them all those picturesque qualities with which they had been invested at the time of my arrival. The father was being reproved, as he emerged upon the porch, for not "slick'n' his ha'r, and wash'n' and fix'n' up, afore hav'n' his pictur' taken;" but the old fellow was obdurate, and joined me in remonstrance against this transformation to the commonplace, on the part of his women-folk. However, there was no profit in arguing with them, and I took my snap-shot with a conviction that the film was being wasted.

We were in several small towns to-day, in pursuance of the policy of distributing our shopping, so as to see as much of the shore

6

life as practicable.   Chief among them have
been New Matamoras (141 miles) and St.
Mary's (154 miles), in West Virginia, and
Newport, in Ohio (155 miles).   Rather dingy
villages, these—each, after their kind, with a
stone wharf thick-grown with weeds; a flour-
ing mill at the head of the landing; a few
cheap-looking, battlemented stores; boys and
men lounging about with that air of comfortable idling which impresses one as the main
characteristic of rustic hamlets, where nobody
seems ever to have anything to do; a ferry
running to the opposite shore—for cattle and
wagons, a heavy flat, with railings, made to
drift with the current; and for foot passengers,
a lumbering skiff, with oars chucking noisily
in their roomy locks.

Every now and then we run across bunches
of oil and gas wells; and great signs, like those
advertising boards which greet railway travelers approaching our large cities, are here and
there perched upon the banks, notifying steamboat pilots, in letters a foot high, that a pipe
line here crosses the river, the vicinity being
consequently unsafe for mooring.

Our camp, to-night, is on a bit of grassy
ledge at the summit of a rocky bank, ten miles

above Marietta, on the Ohio side.   A rod or
so back of us is the country road, which winds
along at the foot of a precipitous steep.   It is
narrow quarters here, and too near the highway for comfort, but nothing better seemed to
offer at the time we needed it; and the outlook
is pleasant, through the fringing oaks and elms,
across the broad river into West Virginia.

We had not yet pitched tent, and all hands
were still clambering over the rocks with Pilgrim's cargo, rather glad that there was no
more of it, when our first camp-bore appeared—a middling-sized man, florid as to
complexion, with a mustache and goatee, and
in a suit of seedy black, surmounted by a
crushed-in Derby hat; and, after the fashion
of the country, giving evidence, on his collarless white shirt, of a free use of chewing tobacco.   I have seldom met a fellow with better
staying qualities.   He was a strawberry grower,
he said, and having been into Newport, a half
dozen miles up river, was walking to his home,
which was a mile or two off in the hills.   Would
we object if, for a few moments, he tarried
here by the roadside? and perhaps we could
accommodate him with a drink of water?   Pa-
tiently did he watch the preparation of dinner,

and spice each dish with commendations of W—'s skill at making the most of her few utensils.

Right glibly he chattered on; now about the decadence of womankind; now about straw-berry-growing upon these Ohio hills—with the crop just coming on, and berries selling at a shilling to-day, in Marietta, when they ought to be worth twenty cents; now on politics, and of course he was a Populist; now on the hard times, and did we believe in free silver? He would take no bite with us, but sat and talked and talked, despite plain hints, growing plainer with the progress of time, that his family needed him at nightfall. Dinner was eaten, and dishes washed; the others left on a botanical round-up, and I produced my writing materials, with remarks upon the lateness of the hour. At last our guest arose, shook the grass from his clothes, with a shake of hands bade me good-night, wishing me to convey his ''good-bye'' to the rest of our party, and as politely as pos-sible expressed the great pleasure which the visit had given him.

Some farmer boys came down the hillside to fish at the bank, and talked pleasantly of their work and of the ever-changing phases of

the river.   Other farmers passed our roadside
door, in wagons, on buckboards, by horseback,
and on foot; in neighborly tone, but with ill-
disguised curiosity in their eyes, wishing me
good evening.   When the long twilight was
almost gone, and the moon an hour high over
the purple dusk of the West Virginia hills, the
botanists returned, aglow with their exercise,
and rich with trophies of blue and dwarf lark-
spur, pink and white stone-crop, trailing ar-
butus, and great laurel.

And then, as we were preparing to retire, a
sleek and dapper fellow, though with clothes
rather the worse for wear, came trudging along
the road toward Marietta.   Seeing our camp,
he asked for a drink.   Being apparently disposed to tarry, the Doctor, to get him started,
offered to walk a piece with him.   Our com-
rade staid out so long, that at last I went down
the road in search of him, and found the pair
sitting on a moonlit bank, as cozily as if they
had been always friends.   The stranger had
revealed to the Doctor that he was a street
fakir, ''by perfesh,'' and had ''struck it rich''
in Chicago during the World's Fair, but somehow had lost the greater part of his gains, and
was now associated with his brother, who had

a junk-boat; the brother was "well heeled,"
and staid and kept store at the boat, while
the fakir, as the walking partner, "rustled
'round 'mong th' grangers, to stir up trade."
The Doctor had, in their talk, let slip something about certain Florida experiences, and
when I arrived on the scene was being skillfully
questioned by his companion as to the proba-
bilities of "a feller o' my perfesh ketch'n' on,
down thar?" The result of this pumping process must have been satisfactory; for when we
parted with him, the fakir declared he was
"go'n' try 't on thar, next winter, 'f I bust me
bottom dollar!"

CHAPTER VIII.

LIFE ASHORE AND AFLOAT—MARIETTA, ''THE
PLYMOUTH RCCK OF THE WEST''—THE
LITTLE KANAWHA—THE STORY OF BLEN-
NERHASSETT'S ISLAND.

BLENNERHASSETT'S ISLAND, Sunday, May
13th.—The day broke without fog, at our
camp on the rocky steep above Marietta. The
eastern sky was veiled with summer clouds, all
gayly flushed by the rising sun, and in the
serene silence of the morning there hung the
scent of dew, and earth, and trees. In the
east, the distant edges of the West Virginia
hills were aglow with the mounting light before
it had yet peeped over into the river trough,
where a silvery haze lent peculiar charm to
flood and bank. Up river, one of the Three
Brothers isles, dark and heavily forested,
seemed in the middle ground to float on air.
A bewitching picture this, until at last the sun
sprang clear and strong above the fringing
hills, and the spell was broken.

The steamboat traffic is improving as we
get lower down.   Last evening, between landing and bedtime, a half dozen passed us, up
and down, breathing heavily as dragons might,
and leaving behind them foamy wakes which
loudly broke upon the shore.   Before morning, I was at intervals awakened by as many
more.   A striking spectacle, the passage of a
big river steamer in the night; you hear, fast
approaching, a labored pant; suddenly, around
the bend, or emerging from behind an island,
the long white monster glides into view,
lanterns gleaming on two lines of deck, her
electric searchlight uneasily flitting to and
fro, first on one landmark, then on another,
her engine bell sharply clanging, the measured
pant developing into a burly, all-pervading
roar, which gradually declines into a pant
again—and then she disappears as she came,
her swelling wake rudely ruffling the moonlit
stream.

We caught up with a large lumber raft this
morning, descending from Pittsburg to Cincinnati.   The half-dozen men in charge were
housed midway in a rude little shanty, and
relieved each other at the sweeps—two at
bow, and two astern.   It is an easy, lounging

life, most of the way, with some difficulties in the shallows, and in passing beneath the great bridges. They travel night and day, except in the not infrequent wind-storms blowing up stream; and it will take them another week to cover the three hundred miles between this and their destination. Far different fellows, these commonplace raftsmen of to-day, from the ''lumber boys'' of a half-century or more ago, when the river towns were regularly "painted red" by the men who followed the Ohio by raft or flatboat. Life along shore was then more picturesque than comfortable.

Later, we stopped on the Ohio shore to chat with a group of farmers having a Sunday talk, their seat a drift log, in the shade of a willowed bank. They proved to be market gardeners and fruit-growers—well-to-do men of their class, and intelligent in conversation; all of them descendants of the sturdy New Englanders who settled these parts.

While the others were discussing small fruits with these transplanted Yankees, who proved quite as full of curiosity about us as we concerning them, I went down shore a hundred yards, struggling through the dense fringe of willows, to photograph a junk-boat just putting off into the stream. The two rough-bearded, merry-eyed fellows at the sweeps were setting their craft broadside to the stream—that "the current might have more holt of her," the chief explained. They were interested in the kodak, and readily posed as I wished, but wanted to see what had been taken, having the common notion that it is like a tintype camera, with results at once attainable. They offered our party a ride for the rest of the day, if we would row alongside and come aboard, but I thanked them, saying their craft was too slow for our needs; at which they laughed heartily, and "'lowed" we might be traders, too, anxious to get in ahead of them—"but there's plenty o' room o' th' river, for yew an' we, stranger! Well, good luck to yees! We'll see yer down below, somewhar, I reckon!"

Just before lunch, we were at Marietta, at the mouth of the Muskingum (171 miles), a fine stream, here two hundred and fifty yards wide. A storied river, this Muskingum. We first definitely hear of it in 1748, the year the original Ohio Company was formed. Céloron was here the year following, with his little band of French soldiers and Indians, vainly endeavoring to turn English traders out of the

Ohio Valley. Christopher Gist came, some months later; then the trader Croghan, for "Old Wyandot Town," the Indian village at the mouth, was a noted center in Western forest traffic. Moravian missionaries appeared in due time, establishing on the banks of the Muskingum the ill-fated convert villages of Schönbrunn, Gnadenhütten, and Salem. In 1785, Fort Harmar was reared on the site of Wyandot Town. Lastly, in the early spring of 1788, came, in Ohio river flatboats, that famous body of New England veterans of the Revolution, under Gen. Rufus Putnam, and planted Marietta—"the Plymouth Rock of the West."

We smile at these Ohio pilgrims, for dignifying the hills which girt in the Marietta bottom, with the names of the seven on which Rome is said to be built—for having a Campus Martius and a Sacra Via, and all that, out here among the sycamore stumps and the wild Indians. But a classical revival was just then vigorously affecting American thought, and it would have been strange if these sturdy New Englanders had not felt its influence, fresh as they were from out the shadows of Harvard and Yale, and in the awesome presence of crowds of huge monumental earthworks, whose

age, in their day, was believed to far outdate
the foundations of the Eternal City itself.
They loved learning for learning's sake; and
here, in the log-cabins of Marietta, eight hundred miles west of their beloved Boston, among
many another good thing they did for poster-
ity, they established the principle of public
education at public cost, as a national principle.

They were soldier colonists. Washington,
out of a full heart, for he dearly loved the
West, said of them: ''No colony in America
was ever settled under such favorable auspices
as that which has just commenced at the Muskingum. Information, property, and strength
will be its characteristics. I know many of
the settlers personally, and there never were
men better calculated to promote the welfare
of such a community." And when, in 1825,
La Fayette had read to him the list of Marietta
pioneers,—nearly fifty military officers among
them,—he cried: ''I know them all! I saw
them at Brandywine, Yorktown, and Rhode
Island. They were the bravest of the brave!"

Yet, for a long time, Marietta met with
small measure of success. Miasma, Indian
ravages, and the conservative temperament of

the people combined to render slow the
growth of this Western Plymouth. There
were, for a time, extensive ship-building yards
here; but that industry gradually declined,
with the growth of railway systems. In our
day, Marietta, with its ten thousand inhabitants, prospers chiefly as a market town and
an educational center, with some manufacturing interests. We were struck to-day, as we
tarried there for an hour or two, with the remarkable resemblance it has in public and
private architecture, and in general tone, to a
typical New England town—say, for example,
Burlington, Vt. Omitting its river front, and
its Mound Cemetery, Marietta might be set
bodily down almost anywhere in Massachusetts, or Vermont, or Connecticut, and the
chance traveler would see little in the place
to remind him of the West. I know of no
other town out of New England of which the
same might be said.

Below Marietta, the river bottoms are, for
miles together, edged with broad stretches of
sloping beach, either deep with sand or naturally paved with pebbles—sometimes treeless,
but often strewn with clumps of willow and
maple and scrub sycamore. The hills, now

rounder, less ambitious, and more widely separated, are checkered with fields and forests, and the bottom lands are of more generous breadth. Pleasant islands stud the peaceful stream. The sylvan foliage has by this time attained very nearly its fullest size. The horse chestnut, the pawpaw, the grape, and the willow are in bloom. A gentle pastoral scene is this through which we glide.

It is evident that it would be a scalding day but for the gentle breeze astern; setting sail, we gladly drop our oars, and, with the water rippling at our prow, sweep blithely down the long southern reach to Parkersburg, W. Va., at the mouth of the Little Kanawha (183 miles). In the full glare of the scorching sun, Parkersburg looks harsh and dry. But it is well built, and, as seen from the river, apparently prosperous. The Ohio is here crossed by the once famous million-dollar bridge of the Baltimore & Ohio railway. The wharf is at the junction of the two streams, but chiefly on the shore of the unattractive Little Kanawha, which is spanned by several bridges, and abounds in steamers and houseboats moored to the land. Clark and Jones did not think well of Little Kanawha lands, yet there were several families

on the river as early as 1763, and Trent,
Croghan, and other Fort Pitt fur-traders had
posts here.   There were only half-a-dozen
houses in 1800, and Parkersburg itself was not
laid out until ten years later.

Blennerhassett's Island lies two miles below—a broad, dark mass of forest, at the head
joined by a dam to the West Virginia shore,
from which it is separated by a slender channel.   Blennerhassett's is some three and a half
miles long; of its five hundred acres, four hundred are under cultivation in three separate
tenant farms.   We landed at the upper end,
where Blennerhassett had his wharf, facing the
Ohio shore, and found that we were tres-
passing upon "The Blennerhassett Pleasure
Grounds."   A seedy-looking man, who represented himself to be the proprietor, promptly
accosted us and levied a "landing fee" of ten
cents per head, which included the right to
remain over night.   A little questioning developed the fact that thirty acres at the head
of the island belong to this man, who rents
the ground to a market gardener,—together
with the comfortable farmhouse which occupies the site of Blennerhassett's mansion,—but
reserves to himself the privilege of levying toll

on visitors. He declared to me that fifteen thousand people came to the island each summer, generally in large railway and steamboat excursions, which gives him an easily-acquired income sufficient for his needs. It is a pity that so famous a place is not a public park.

The touching story of the Blennerhassetts is one of the best known in Western annals. Rich in culture and worldly possessions, but wildly impracticable, Harman Blennerhassett and his beautiful wife came to America in 1798. Buying this lovely island in the Ohio, six hundred miles west of tidewater, they built a large mansion, which they furnished luxuriously, adorning it with fine pictures and statuary. Here, in the midst of beautiful grounds, while Blennerhassett studied astronomy, chemistry, and galvanism, his brilliant spouse dispensed rare hospitality to their many distinguished guests; for, in those days, it was part of a rich young man's education to take a journey down the Ohio, into "the Western parts," and on returning home to write a book about it.

But there came a serpent to this Eden. Aaron Burr was among their visitors (1805), while upon his journey to New Orleans, where he hoped to set on foot a scheme to seize either Texas or Mexico, and set up a republic with himself at the head. He interested the susceptible Blennerhassetts in his plans, the import of which they probably little understood; but the fantastic Englishman had suffered a considerable reduction of fortune, and was anxious to recoup, and Burr's representations were aglow with the promise of such rewards in the golden southwest as Cortes and Coronado sought. Blennerhassett's purse was opened to the enterprise of Burr; large sums were spent in boats and munitions, which were, tradition says, for a time hid in the bayou which, close by our camp, runs deep into the island forest. It has been filled in by the present proprietor, but its bold shore lines, all hung with giant sycamores, are still in evidence.

President Jefferson's proclamation (October, 1806) shattered the plot, and Blennerhassett fled to join Burr at the mouth of the Cumberland. Both were finally arrested (1807), and tried for treason, but acquitted on technical grounds. In the meantime, people from the neighboring country sacked Blennerhassett's house; then came creditors, and with great

7

waste seized his property; the beautiful place was still further pillaged by lawless ruffians, and turned into ignoble uses; later, the mansion itself was burned through the carelessness of negroes—and now, all they can show us are the old well and the noble trees which once graced the lawn. As for the Blennerhassetts themselves, they wandered far and wide, everywhere the victims of misfortune. He died on the Island of Guernsey (1831), a disappointed office-seeker; she, returning to America to seek redress from Congress for the spoliation of her home, passed away in New York, before the claim was allowed, and was buried by the Sisters of Charity.

CHAPTER IX.

POOR WHITES—FIRST LIBRARY IN THE WEST—
AN HOUR AT HOCKINGPORT—A HERMIT
FISHER.

LONG BOTTOM, Monday, May 14th.—Pushing up stream for two miles this morning, the
commissary department replenished the day's
stores at Parkersburg. Forepaugh's circus
was in town, and crowds of rustics were coming in by wagon road, railway trains, and
steamers and ferries on both rivers. The
streets of the quaint, dingy Southern town
were teeming with humanity, mainly negroes
and poor whites. Among the latter, flat,
pallid faces, either flabby or too lean, were
under the swarms of blue, white, and yellow
sunbonnets—sad faces, with lack-luster eyes,
coarse hair of undecided hue, and coarser
speech. These Audreys of Dixie-land are the
product of centuries of ill-treatment on our
soil; indented white servants to the early coast
colonists were in the main their ancestors;

with slave competition, the white laborer in the South lost caste until even the negro despised him; and ill-nurture has done the rest. Then, too, in these bottoms, malaria has wrought its work, especially among the underfed; you see it in the yellow skin and nerveless tone of these lanky rustics, who are in town to enjoy the one bright holiday of their weary year.

Across the river, in Ohio, is Belpré (short for Belle Prairie, and now locally pronounced Bel pry), settled by Revolutionary soldiers, on the Marietta grant, in 1789-90. I always think well of Belpré, because here was established the first circulating library in the Northwest. Old Israel Putnam, he of the wolf-den and Bunker Hill, amassed many books. His son Israel, on moving to Belpré in 1796, carried a considerable part of the collection with him—no small undertaking this, at a time when goods had to be carted all the way from Connecticut, over rivers and mountains to the Ohio, and then floated down river by flatboat, with a high tariff for every pound of freight. Young Israel was public-spirited, and, having been at so great cost and trouble to get this library out to the wilderness, desired his fellow-colonists to en-

joy it with him.   It would have been unfair
not to distribute the expense, so a stock company was formed, and shares were sold at ten
dollars each.   Of the blessings wrought in
this rude frontier community by the books
which the elder Israel had collected for his
Connecticut fireside, there can be no more
eloquent testimony than that borne by an old
settler, who, in 1802, writes to an Eastern
friend: ''In order to make the long winter
evenings pass more smoothly, by great exer-
tion I purchased a share in the Belpré library,
six miles distant.   Many a night have I passed
(using pine knots instead of candles) reading
to my wife while she sat hatcheling, carding
or spinning.''   The association was dissolved
in 1815 or 1816, and the books distributed
among the shareholders; many of these volumes are still extant in this vicinity, and several are in the college museum at Marietta.

There are few descendants hereabout of the
original New England settlers, and they live
miles apart on the Ohio shore.   We went up
to visit one, living opposite Blennerhassett's
Island.   Notice of our coming had preceded
us, and we were warmly welcomed at a substantial farmhouse in the outskirts of Belpré,

with every evidence about of abundant prosperity. The maternal great-grandfather of our host for an hour was Rufus Putnam, an ancestor to be proud of. Five acres of gooseberries are grown on the place, and other small-fruits in proportion—all for the Parkersburg market, whence much is shipped north to Cleveland. Our host confessed to a little malaria, even on this upper terrace—or "second bottom," as they style it—but "the land is good, though with many stones—natural conditions, you know, for New Englanders." It was pleasant for a New England man, not long removed from his native soil, to find these people, who are a century away from home, still claiming kinship.

At the Big Hockhocking River (197 miles), on a high, semicircular bottom, is Hockingport, a hamlet with a population of three hundred. Here, on a still higher bench, a quarter of a mile back from the river, Lord Dunmore built Fort Gower, one of a chain of posts along his march against the Northwest Indians (1774). It was from here that he marched to the Pickaway Plains, on the Scioto (near Circleville, O.), and concluded that treaty of peace to which Chief Logan refused

his consent.   There are some remains yet left
of this palisaded earthwork of a century and
a quarter ago, but the greater part has been
obliterated by plowing, and a dwelling occupies a portion of the site.

It had been very warm, and we had needed
an awning as far down as Hockingport, where
we cooled off by lying on the grass in the
shade of the village blacksmith's shop, which
is, as well, the ferry-house, with the bell hung
between two tall posts at the top of the bank,
its rope dangling down for public use.   The
smith-ferryman came out with his wife—a
burly, good-natured couple—and joined us in
our lounging, for it is not every day that
river travelers put in at this dreamy, far-
away port.   The wife had camped with her
husband, when he was boss of a railway con-
struction gang, and both of them frankly en-
vied us our trip.   So did a neighboring store-
keeper, a tall, lean, grave young man, clean-
shaven, coatless and vestless, with a blue-
glass stud on his collarless white shirt.   Apparently there was no danger of customers
walking away with his goods, for he left his
store-door open to all comers, not once glancing thitherward in the half-hour he sat with

us on a stick of timber, in which he pensively carved his name.

Life goes easily in Hockingport. Years ago there was some business up the Big Hocking (short for Big Hockhocking), a stream of a half-dozen rods' width, but now no steamer ventures up—the railroads do it all; as for the Ohio—well, the steamers now and then put off a box or bale for the four shop-keepers, and once in a while a passenger patronizes the landing. There is still a little country traffic, and formerly a sawmill was in operation here; you see its ruins down there below. Hockingport is a type of several rustic hamlets we have seen to-day; they are often in pairs, one either side of the river, for companionship's sake.

We are idling, despite the knowledge that on turning every big bend we are getting farther and farther south, and mid-June on the Lower Ohio is apt to be sub-tropical. But the sinking sun gives us a shadowy right bank, and that is most welcome. The current is only spasmodically good. Every night the river falls from three to six inches, and there are long stretches of slack-water. The steamers pick their way carefully; we do not give them

as wide a berth as formerly, for the wakes
they turn are no longer savage—but wakes,
even when sent out by stern-wheelers at full
speed, now give us little trouble; it did not
take long to learn the knack of "taking"
them.   Whether you meet them at right angles, or in the trough, there is the same delicious sensation of rising and falling on the
long swells—there is no danger, so long as
you are outside the line of foaming breakers;
within those, you may ship water, which is
not desirable when there is a cargo.   But the
boys at the towns sometimes put out in their
rude punts into the very vortex of disturbance, being dashed about in the white roar
at the base of the ponderous paddle wheels,
like a Fiji Islander in his surf-boat.   We heard,
the other day, of a boatload of daring young-
sters being caught by the wheel, their craft
smashed into kindling-wood, and they themselves all drowned but one.

The hills, to-day, sometimes break sharply
off, leaving an eroded, often vine-festooned palisade some fifty feet in height, at the base of
which is a long, tree-clad slope of debris;
then, a narrow, level terrace from fifty to a
hundred yards in width, which drops suddenly

to a rocky beach; this in turn is often lined
along the water's edge with irregularly-shaped
boulders, from the size of Pilgrim to fifteen
or twenty feet in height, and worn smooth
with the grinding action of the river. The
effect is highly picturesque. We shall have
much of this below.

At the foot of one of these palisades lay a
shanty-boat, with nets sprawled over the roof
to dry, and a live-box anchored hard by.
"Hello, the boat!" brought to the window
the head of the lone fisherman, who dreamily
peered at us as we announced our wish to become his customers. A sort of poor-white
Neptune, this tall, lean, lantern-jawed old
fellow, with great round, iron-rimmed spectacles over his fishy eyes, his hair and beard
in long, snaky locks, and clothing in dirty tatters. As he put out in his skiff to reach the
live-box, he continuously spewed tobacco juice
about him, and in an undertone growled gar-
rulously, as though used to soliloquize in his
hermitage, where he lay at outs with the
world. He had been in this spot for two
years, he said, and sold fish to the daily Parkersburg steamer—when there were any fish.
But, for six months past, he "hadn't made

enough to keep him in grub," and had now and then to go up to the city and earn something. For forty years had he followed the apostles' calling on "this yere Ohio," and the fishing was never so poor as now—yes, sir! hard times had struck his business, just like other folks'. He thought the oil wells were tainting the water, and the fish wouldn't breed—and the iron slag, too, was spoiling the river, and he knew it. He finally produced for us, out of his box, a three-pound fish,—white perch, calico bass, and catfish formed his stock in trade,—but, before handing it over, demanded the requisite fifteen cents. Evidently he had had dealings with a dishonest world, this hermit fisher, and had learned a thing or two.

Perfect camping places are not to be found every day. There are so many things to think of—a good landing place; good height above the water level, in case of a sudden rise; a dry, shady, level spot for the tent; plenty of wood, and, if possible, a spring; and not too close proximity to a house. Occasionally we meet with what we want, when we want it; but quite as often, ideal camping places, while abundant half the day, are not to be found at five o'clock, our usual hour for homeseeking. The Doctor is our agent for this task, for, being bow oar, he can clamber out most easily. This evening, he ranged both shores for a considerable distance, with ill success, so that we are settled on a narrow Ohio sand-beach, in the midst of a sparse willow copse, only two feet above the river. Dinner was had at the very water's edge. After a time, a wind-storm arose and flapped the tent right vigorously, causing us to pin down tightly and weight the sod-cloth; while, amid distant thundering, every preparation was made for a speedy embarkation in the event of flood. The bellow of the frogs all about us, the scream of toads, and the heavy swash of passing steamers dangerously near our door, will be a sufficient lullaby to-night.

CHAPTER X.

CLIFF-DWELLERS ON LONG BOTTOM — POM-
EROY BEND—LETART'S ISLAND AND RAP-
IDS — GAME IN THE EARLY DAY—RAINY
WEATHER—IN A ''CRACKER'' HOME.

LETART'S ISLAND, Tuesday, May 15th.—
After we had gone to bed last night,—we in
the tent, the Doctor and Pilgrim under the fly,
which serves as a porch roof,—the heavenly
floodgates lifted; the rain, coming in sheets,
beat a fierce tattoo on the tightly-stretched
canvas, and visions of a sudden rise in the
fickle river were uppermost in our dreams.
Everything about us was sopping at daybreak;
but the sun rose clear and warm from a bed
of eastern clouds, and the midnight gale had
softened to a gentle breeze.

Palisades were frequent to-day. We stopped
just below camp, at an especially picturesque
Ohio hamlet,—Long Bottom (207 miles),—
where the dozen or so cottages are built close
against the bald rock. Clambering over great
water-worn boulders, at the river's brink, the

Doctor and I made our way up through a
dense tangle of willows and poison ivy and
grape-vines, emerging upon the country road
which passes at the foot of this row of modern
cliff-dwellings.   For the most part, little gardens, with neat palings, run down from the
cottages to the road.   One sprawling log house,
fairly embowered in vines, and overtopped by
the palisade rising sheer for thirty feet above
its back door, looked in this setting for all the
world like an Alpine chalet, lacking only stones
on the roof to complete the picture.   I took a
kodak shot at this, also at a group of tousle-
headed children at the door of a decrepit shanty
built entirely within a crevice of the rock—
their Hibernian mother, with one hand holding
an apron over her head, and the other shield-
ing her eyes, shrilly crying to a neighboring
cliff-dweller: "Miss McCarthy! Miss Mc-
Carthy! There's a feller here, a photergraph'n'
all the people in the Bottom! Come, quick!"
Then they eagerly pressed around me, Germans and Irish, big and little, women and
children mostly, asking for a view of the
picture, which I gave all in turn by letting
them peep into the ground-glass "finder"—a
pretty picture, they said it was, with the colors

all in, and "wonderfully like," though a wee bit small.

Speaking of color, we are daily struck with the brilliant hues in the workaday dresses of women and children seen along the river.   Red calico predominates, but blues and yellows, and even greens, are seen, brightly splashing the somber landscape.

After Long Bottom, we enter upon the south-sweeping Pomeroy Bend of the Ohio, commencing at Murraysville (208 miles) and ending at Pomeroy (247 miles).   It is of itself a series of smaller bends, and, as we twist about upon our course, the wind strikes us successively on all quarters; sometimes giving the Doctor a chance to try his sail, which he raises on the slightest provocation,—but at all times agreeably ruffling the surface that would otherwise reflect the glowing sun like a mirror.

The sloping margins of the rich bottoms are now often cultivated almost to the very edge of the stream, with a line of willow trees left as a protecting fringe.   Farmers doing this take a gambling risk of a summer rise.   Where the margins have been left untouched by the plow, there is a dense mass of vegetation—

sycamores, big of girth and towering to a hundred feet or more, abound on every hand; the willows are phenomenally-rapid growers; and in all available space is the rank, thick-standing growth of an annual locally styled ''horseweed,'' which rears a cane-like stalk full eighteen or twenty feet high—it has now attained but four or five feet, but the dry stalks of last year's growth are everywhere about, showing what a formidable barrier to landing these giant weeds must be in midsummer.

We chose for a camping place Letart's Island (232 miles), on the West Virginia side, not far below Milwood. From the head, where our tent is pitched on a sandy knoll thick-grown to willows, a long gravel spit runs far over toward the Ohio shore. The West Virginia channel is narrow, slow and shallow; that between us and Ohio has been lessened by the island to half its usual width, and the current sweeps by at a six-mile gait, in which the Doctor and I found it difficult to keep our footing while having our customary evening dip. Our island is two long, forested humps of sand, connected by a stretch of gravel beach, giving every evidence of being submerged in times of flood; everywhere are chaotic heaps of driftwood, many cords in extent; derelict trees are lodged in the tops of the highest willows and maples—ghostly giants sprawling in the moonlight; there is an abandon of vegetable debris, layer after layer laid down in sandy coverlids.   Wild grasses, which flourish on all these flooded lands, here attain enormous size. Dispensing with our cots for the nonce, we have spread our blankets over heaps of dried grass pulled from the monster tufts of last year's growth.   The Ohio is capable of raising giant floods; it is still falling with us, but there are signs at hand, beyond the slight sprinkle which cooled the air for us at bedtime, of rainy weather after the long drouth.   When the feeders in the Alleghanies begin to swell, we shall perch high o' nights.

NEAR CHESHIRE, O., Wednesday, May 16th.—The fine current at the island gave us a noble start this morning.   The river soon widens, but Letart's Falls, a mile or two below, continue the movement, and we went fairly spinning on our way.   These so-called falls, rapids rather, long possessed the imagination of early travelers.   Some of the chroniclers have, while describing them, indulged in

8

flights of fancy.* They are of slight consequence, however, even at this low stage of
water, save to the careless canoeist who has
had no experience in rapid water, well-strewn
with sunken boulders. The scenery of the
locality is wild, and somewhat impressive.
The Ohio bank is steep and rugged, abounding
in narrow little terraces of red clay, deeply
gullied, and dotted with rough, mean shanties.
It all had a forbidding aspect, when viewed in
the blinding sun; but before we had passed, an
intervening cloud cast a deep shadow over the
scene, and, softening the effect, made the
picture more pleasing.

Croghan was at Letart (1765), on one of
his land-viewing trips for the Ohio Company,
and tells us that he saw a "vast migrating
herd" of buffalo cross the river here. In the
beginning of colonization in this valley, buffalo
and elk were to be seen in herds of astonishing
size; traces of their well-beaten paths through
the hills, and toward the salt licks of Kentucky

---

* Notably, Ashe's *Travels;* but Palmer, while saying that
"they are the only obstruction to the navigation of the Ohio,
except the rapids at Louisville," declares them to be of slight
difficulty, and, referring to Ashe's account, says, "Like great
part of his book, it is all romance."

and Illinois, were observable until within re-
cent years.   Gordon, an early traveler down
the Ohio (1766), speaks of "great herds of
buffalo, we observed on the beaches of the
river and islands into which they come for air,
and coolness in the heat of the day;" he commenced his raids on them a hundred miles
below Pittsburg.   Hutchins (1778) says, "the
whole country abounds in Bears, Elks, Buf-
faloe, Deer, Turkies, &c."*   Bears, panthers,
wolves, eagles, and wild turkeys were indeed
very plenty at first, but soon became extinct.
The theory is advanced by Dr. Doddridge, in
his *Notes on Virginia*, that hunters' dogs introduced hydrophobia among the wolves, and
this ridded the country of them sooner than
they would naturally have gone; but they were
still so numerous in 1817, that the traveler
Palmer heard them nightly, "barking on both
banks."

Venomous serpents were also numerous in
pioneer days, and stayed longer.   The story is
told of a tumulus up toward Moundsville, that

---

* The last buffalo on record, in the Upper Ohio region,
was killed in the Great Kanawha Valley, a dozen miles from
Charleston, W. Va., in 1815.   Five years later, in the same
vicinity, was killed probably the last elk seen east of the Ohio.

abounded in snakes, particularly rattlers. The settlers thought to dig them out, but they came to such a mass of human bones that that plan was abandoned. Then they instituted a blockade, by erecting a tight-board fence around the mound, and, thus entrapping the reptiles, extirpated the colony in a few days.

Paroquets were once abundant west of the Alleghanies, up to the southern shore of the Great Lakes, and great flocks haunted the salt springs; but to-day they may be found only in the middle Southern states. There were, in a state of nature, no crows, blackbirds, or song-birds in this valley; they followed in the wake of the colonist. The honey bee came with the white man,—or rather, just preceded him. Rats followed the first settlers, then opossums, and fox squirrels still later. It is thought, too, that the sand-hill and whooping cranes, and the great blue herons which we daily see in their stately flight, are birds of these later days, when the neighborhood of man has frightened away the enemies which once kept them from thriving in the valley. Turkey buzzards appear to remain alone of the ancient birds; the earliest travelers note their presence in great flocks, and to-day there

are few vistas open to us, without from one to
dozens of them wheeling about in mid-air,
seeking what they may devour.   Public opinion
in the valley is opposed to the wanton killing
of these scavengers, so useful in a climate as
warm as this.

Three miles below Letart's Rapids, is the
motley settlement of Antiquity, O., a long row
of cabins and cottages nestled at the base of a
high, vine-clad palisade, similar to that which
yesterday we visited at Long Bottom.   Some
of these cliff-dwellings are picturesque, some
exhibit the prosperity of their owners, but
many are squalid.   At the water's edge is that
which has given its name to the locality, an
ancient rock, which once bore some curious
Indian carving.   Hall (1820) found only one
figure remaining, ''a man in a sitting posture,
making a pipe;'' to-day, even thus much has
been largely obliterated by the elements.   But
Antiquity itself is not quite dead.   There is a
ship-yard here; and a sawmill in active operation, besides the ruins of two others.

We also passed Racine (240 miles), another
Ohio town—a considerable place, no doubt,
although only the tops of the buildings were,
from the river level, to be seen above the high

bank; these, and an enticing view up the
wharf-street.   Of more immediate interest,
just then, were the heavens, now black and
threatening.   Putting in hurriedly to the West
Virginia shore, we pitched tent on a shelving
clay beach, shielded by the ever-present willows, and in five minutes had everything under
shelter.   With a rumble and bang, and a great
flurry of wind, the thunder-storm broke upon
us in full fury.   There had been no time to
run a ditch around the tent, so we spread our
cargo atop of the cots.   The Boy engineered
riverward the streams of water which flowed
in beneath the canvas; W—, ever practical,
caught rain from the dripping fly, and did the
family washing, while the Doctor and I prepared a rather pasty lunch.

An hour later, we bailed out Pilgrim, and
once more ventured upon our way.   It is a
busy district between Racine and Sheffield
(251 miles).   For eleven miles, upon the Ohio
bank, there are few breaks between the
towns,—Racine, Syracuse, Minersville, Pomeroy, Coalport, Middleport, and Sheffield.
Coal mines and salt works abound, with other
industries interspersed; and the neighborhood
appears highly prosperous.   Its metropolis is

Pomeroy, in shape a "shoe-string" town,—
much of it not over two blocks wide, and
stretching along for two miles, at the foot of
high palisades.   West Virginia is not far behind, in enterprise, with the salt-work towns
of New Haven, Hartford, and Mason City,—
bespeaking, in their names, a Connecticut
ancestry.

The afternoon sun gushed out, and the face
of Nature was cleanly beautiful, as, leaving
the convolutions of the Pomeroy Bend, we
entered upon that long river-sweep to the
south-by-southwest, which extends from Pomeroy to the Big Sandy, a distance of sixty-
eight miles.   A mile or two below Cheshire,
O. (256 miles), we put in for the night on the
West Virginia shore.   There is a natural pier
of rocky ledge, above that a sloping beach of
jagged stone, and then the little grassy terrace
which we have made our home.

Searching for milk and eggs, I walked along
a railway track and then up through a cornfield, to a little log farm-house, whose broad
porch was shingled with "shakes" and shaded
by a lusty grape-vine.   Fences, house, and out-
buildings had been newly whitewashed, and
there was all about an uncommon air of neat-

ness. A stout little girl of eleven or twelve, met me at the narrow gate opening through the garden palings. It may be because a gypsying trip like this roughens one in many ways,—for man, with long living near to Nature's heart, becomes of the earth, earthy,— that she at first regarded me with suspicious eyes, and, with one hand resting gracefully on her hip, parleyed over the gate, as to what price I was paying in cash, for eggs and milk, and where I hailed from.

With her wealth of blond hair done up in a saucy knot behind; her round, honest face; her lips thick, and parted over pearly teeth; her nose saucily *retrousse;* and her flashing, outspoken blue eyes, this barefooted child of Nature had a certain air of authority, a consciousness of power, which made her womanly beyond her years. She must have seen that I admired her, this little "cracker" queen, in her clean but tattered calico frock; for her mood soon melted, and with much grace she ushered me within the house. Calling Sam, an eight-year-old, to "keep the gen'lem'n comp'ny," she prettily excused herself, and scampered off up the hillside in search of the cows.

A barefooted, loose-jointed, gaunt, sandy-

haired, freckled, open-eyed youngster is Sam.
He came lounging into the room, and, taking
my hat, hung it on a peg above the fireplace;
then, dropping into a big rocking-chair, with
his muddy legs hanging over an arm, at once,
with a curious, old-fashioned air, began "keeping company" by telling me of the new litter
of pigs, with as little diffidence as though I
were an old neighbor who had dropped in on
the way to the cross-roads. "And thet thar
new Shanghai rooster, mister, ain't he a beauty?
He cost a dollar, he did—a dollar in silver,
sir!"

There was no difficulty in drawing Sam
out. He is frankness itself. What was he
going to make of himself? Well, he "'lowed"
he wanted to be either a locomotive engineer
or a steamboat captain—hadn't made up his
mind which. "But whatever a boy wants
to be, he will be!" said Sam, with the decided
tone of a man of the world, who had seen
things. I asked Sam what the attractions
were in the life of an engine driver. He
"'lowed" they went so fast through the world,
and saw so many different people; and in
their lifetime served on different roads, maybe,
and surely they must meet with some excite-

ment.   And in that of a steamboat captain?
"Oh! now yew're talk'n', mister!   A right
smart business, thet!   A boss'n' o' people
'round, a seein' o' th' world, and noth'n' 't all
to do!   Now, that's right smart, I take it!"
It was plain where his heart lay.   He saw the
steamers pass the farm daily, and once he
had watched one unload at Point Pleasant—
well, that was the life for him!   Sam will
have to be up and doing, if he is to be the
monarch of a stern-wheeler on the Ohio; but
many another "cracker" boy has attained
this exalted station, and Sam is of the sort to
win his way.

Soon the kine came lowing into the yard,
and my piquant young friend who had met
me at the gate stood in the doorway talking
with us both, while their brother Charley, an
awkward, self-conscious lad of ten, took my
pail and milked into it the required two
quarts.   It is a large, square room, where I
was so agreeably entertained.   The well-
chinked logs are scrupulously whitewashed;
the parental bed, with gay pillow shams,
bought from a peddler, occupies one corner;
a huge brick fireplace opens black and yawning, into the base of a great cobblestone

chimney reared against the house without,
after the fashion of the country; on pegs
about, hang the best clothes of the family;
while a sewing-machine, a deal table, a cheap
little mirror as big as my palm, a few un-
framed chromos, and a gaudy "Family Record" chart hung in an old looking-glass
frame,—with appropriate holes for tintypes of
father, mother and children,—complete the
furnishings of the apartment, which is parlor,
sitting-room, dining-room, and bedroom all in
one.

My little queen was evidently proud of her
throne-room, and noted with satisfaction my
interest in the Family Record.   When I had
paid her for butter and eggs, at retail rates,
she threw in an extra egg, and, despite my
protests, would have Charley take the pail out
to the cow, "for an extra squirt or two, for
good measure!"

I was bidding them all good-bye, and the
queen was pressing me to come again in the
morning "fer more stuff, ef ye 'lowed yew
wanted any," when the mother of the little
brood appeared from over the fields, where
she had been to carry water to her lord.   A
fair, intelligent, rather fine-looking woman,

but barefooted like the rest; from her neck
behind, dangled a red sunbonnet, and a
sunny-haired child of five was in her arms—
''sort o' weak in her lungs, poor thing!'' she
sadly said, as I snapped my fingers at the
smiling tot. I tarried a moment with the
good mother, as, sitting upon the porch, she
serenely smiled upon her children, whose eyes
were now lit with responsive love; and I
wondered if there were not some romance
hidden here, whereby a dash of gentler blood
had through this sweet-tempered woman been
infused into the coarse clay of the bottom.

CHAPTER XI.

BATTLE OF POINT PLEASANT—THE STORY OF
GALLIPOLIS — ROSEBUD — HUNTINGTON —
THE GENESIS OF A HOUSE-BOATER.

NEAR GLENWOOD, W. VA., Thursday, May
17th.—By eight o'clock this morning we were
in Point Pleasant, W. Va., at the mouth of
the Great Kanawha River (263 miles). Céloron was here, the eighteenth of August, 1749,
and on the east bank of the river, the site of
the present village, buried at the foot of an
elm one of his leaden plates asserting the claim
of France to the Ohio basin. Ninety-seven
years later, a boy unearthed this interesting
but futile proclamation, and it rests to-day in
the museum of the Virginia Historical Society.

The Great Kanawha Valley long had a
romantic interest for Englishmen concerned
in Western lands. It was in the grant to
the old Ohio Company; but that corporation,
handicapped in many ways, was practically
dead by the time of Lord Dunmore's war.

It had many rivals, more or less ephemeral, among them the scheme of George Mercer (1773) to have the territory between the Alleghanies and the Ohio—the West Virginia of to-day—erected into the "Province of Vandalia," with himself as governor, and his capital at the mouth of the Great Kanawha. Washington owned a ten-thousand-acre tract on both sides of the river, commencing a short distance above the mouth, which he surveyed in person, in October, 1770; and in 1773 we find him advertising to sell or lease it; among the inducements he offered was, "the scheme for establishing a new government on the Ohio," and the contiguity of his lands "to the seat of government, which, it is more than probable, will be fixed at the mouth of the Great Kanawha." Had not the Revolution broken out, and nipped this and many another budding plan for Western colonization, there is little doubt that what we call West Virginia would have been established as a state, a century earlier than it was.*

---

* Washington was much interested in a plan to connect, by a canal, the James and Great Kanawha Rivers, separated at their sources by a portage of but a few miles in length.

A few days ago we were at Mingo Bottom,
where lived Chief Logan, whose family were
treacherously slaughtered by border ruffians
(1774). The Mingos, ablaze with the fire of
vengeance, carried the war-pipe through the
neighboring villages; runners were sent in
every direction to rouse the tribes; tomahawks
were unearthed, war-posts were planted; mes-
sages of defiance sent to the Virginians; and
in a few days Lord Dunmore's war was in full
swing, from Cumberland Gap to Fort Pitt,
from the Alleghanies to the Wabash.

His lordship, then governor of Virginia, was
full of energy, and proved himself a compe-
tent military manager. The settlers were organized; the rude log forts were garrisoned;
forays were made against the Indian villages
as far away as Muskingum, and an army of

The distance from Point Pleasant to Richmond is 485 miles.
In 1785, Virginia incorporated the James River Company,
of which Washington was the first president. The project
hung fire, because of "party spirit and sectional jealousies,"
until 1832, when a new company was incorporated, under
which the James was improved (1836-53), but the Kanawha
was untouched. In 1874, United States engineers presented
a plan calling for an expenditure of sixty millions, but there
the matter rests. The Kanawha is navigable by large
steamers for sixty miles, up to the falls at Charleston, and
beyond almost to its source, by light craft.

nearly three thousand backwoodsmen, armed with smooth-bores and clad in fringed buckskin hunting-shirts, was put in the field.

One division of this army, eleven hundred strong, under Gen. Andrew Lewis, descended the Great Kanawha River, and on Point Pleasant met Cornstalk, a famous Shawnee chief, who, while at first peaceful, had by the Logan tragedy been made a fierce enemy of the whites, and was now the leader of a thousand picked warriors, gathered from all parts of the Northwest. On the 10th of October, from dawn until dusk, was here waged in a gloomy forest one of the most bloody and stubborn hand-to-hand battles ever fought between Indians and whites—especially notable, too, because for the first time the rivals were about equal in number. The combatants stood behind trees, in Indian fashion, and it is hard to say who displayed the best generalship, Cornstalk or Lewis. * When the pall of night cov-

---

* Hall, in *Romance of Western History* (1820), says that when Washington was tendered command of the Revolutionary army, he replied that it should rather be given to Gen. Andrew Lewis, of whose military abilities he had a high opinion. Lewis was a captain in the Little Meadows affair (1752), and a companion of Washington in Braddock's defeat (1755).

ered the hideous contest, the whites had lost one-fifth of their number, while the savages had sustained but half as many casualties. Cornstalk's followers had had enough, however, and withdrew before daylight, leaving the field to the Americans.

A few days later, General Lewis joined Lord Dunmore—who headed the other wing of the army, which had proceeded by the way of Forts Pitt and Gower — on the Pickaway plains, in Ohio; and there a treaty was made with the Indians, who assented to every proposition made them. They surrendered all claim to lands south of the Ohio River, returned their white prisoners and stolen horses, and gave hostages for future good behavior.

Here at Point Pleasant, a year later, Fort Randolph was built, and garrisoned by a hundred men; for, despite the treaty, the Indians were still troublesome. For a long time, Pittsburg, Redstone, and Randolph were the only garrisoned forts on the frontier. The Point Pleasant of to-day is a dull, sleepy town of twenty-five hundred inhabitants, with that unkempt air and preponderance of lounging negroes, so common to small Southern communities. The bottom is rolling, fringed with

9

large hills, and on the Ohio side drops suddenly for fifty feet to a shelving beach of gravel and clay.   Crooked Creek, in whose narrow, winding valley some of the severest fighting was had, empties into the Kanawha a half-mile up the stream, at the back of the town.   It was painful to meet several men of intelligence, who had long been engaged in trade here, to whom the Battle of Point Pleasant was a shadowy event, whose date they could not fix, nor whose importance understand; it seemed to be little more a part of their lives, than an obscure contest between Matabeles and whites, in far-off Africa.   It is time that our Western and Southern folk were awakened to an appreciation of the fact that they have a history at their doors, quite as significant in the annals of civilization as that which induces pilgrimages to Ticonderoga and Bunker Hill.

Four miles below, Pilgrim was beached for a time at Gallipolis, O. (267 miles), which has a story all its own.   The district belonged, a century ago, to the Scioto Company, an offshoot of the Marietta enterprise.   Joel Barlow, the "poet of the Revolution," was sent to Paris (May, 1788) as agent for the sale of lands.   As the result of his personal popularity there, and his flaming immigration circulars and maps, he disposed of a hundred thousand acres; to settle on which, six hundred French emigrants sailed for America, in February, 1790. They were peculiarly unsuited for colonization, even under the most favorable conditions—being in the main physicians, jewelers and other artisans, a few mechanics, and noblemen's servants, while many were without trade or profession.

Upon arrival in Alexandria, Va., they found that their deeds were valueless, the land never having been paid for by the Scioto speculators; moreover, the tract was filled with hostile Indians. However, five hundred of them pushed on to the region, by way of Redstone, and reached here by flatboat, in a destitute condition. The Marietta neighbors were as kind as circumstances would allow, and cabins were built for them on what is now the Public Square of Gallipolis. But they were ignorant of the first principles of forestry or gardening; the initial winter was exceptionally severe, Indian forays sapped the life of the colony, yellow fever decimated the survivors; and, altogether, the little settlement suffered a series of disasters almost unparalleled in the story of American colonization.

Although finally reimbursed by Congress with a special land grant, the emigrants gradually died off, until now, so at least we were assured, but three families of descendants of the original Gauls are now living here.   It was the American element, aided by sturdy Germans, who in time took hold of the decayed French settlement, and built up the prosperous little town of six thousand inhabitants which we find to-day.   It is a conservative town, with little perceptible increase in population; but there are many fine brick blocks, the stores have large stocks attractively displayed, and there is in general a comfortable tone about the place, which pleases a stranger.   The Public Square, where the first Gauls had their little forted town, appears to occupy the space of three or four city blocks; there is the customary band-stand in the center, and seats plentifully provided along the graveled walks which divide neat plots of grass.   Over the riverward entrance to the square, is an arch of gas-pipe, perforated for illumination, and bearing the dates, "1790-1890,"—a relic, this, of

the centennial which Gallipolis celebrated in
the last-named year.

It was with some difficulty that we found a
camping-place, this evening. For several
miles, the approaches were nearly knee-deep in
mud for a dozen feet back from the water's edge,
or else the banks were too steep, or the farmers had cultivated so closely to the brink as to
leave us no room for the tent. In one gruesome spot on the Ohio bank, where a projecting log fortunately served as a pier, the Doctor
landed for a prospecting tour; while I ascended
a zigzag path, through steep and rugged land,
to a nest of squalid cabins perched by a shabby
hillside road. A vicious dog came down to
meet me half-way, and might have succeeded
in carrying off a portion of my clothing had
not his owner whistled him back.

A queer, dingy, human wasp-nest, this dirty
little shanty hamlet of Rosebud. Pigs and
children wallowed in comradeship, and as every
cabin on the precipitous slope necessarily has
a basement, this is used as the common barn
for chickens, goats, pigs, and cow. It was
pleasant to find that there was no sweet milk
to be had in Rosebud, for it is kept in open
pans, in these fetid rooms, and soon sours—

and the cows had not yet come down from the
hills.   Water, too, was at a premium.   There
was none to be had, save what had fallen from
the clouds, and been stored in a foul cistern,
which seemed common property.   I drew a
pailful of it, not to displease the disheveled
group which surrounded me, full of questions;
but on the first turning in the lane, emptied
the vessel upon the back of a pig, which was
darting by with murderous squeal.

The long twilight was well nigh spent, when,
on the Ohio side a mile or two above Glenwood, W. Va. (287 miles), we came upon a
wide, level beach of gravel, below a sloping,
willowed terrace, above which sharply rose
the "second bottom."   Ascending an angling
farm roadway, while the others pitched camp,
I walked over the undulating bottom to the
nearest of a group of small, neat farmhouses,
and applied for milk.   While a buxom maid
went out and milked a Jersey, that had chanced
to come home ahead of her fellows, I sat on
the rear porch gossiping with the farm-wife—
a Pennsylvania-Dutch dame of ample propor-
tions, attired in light-blue calico, and with
huge spectacles over her broad, flat nose.
She and her "man" own a hundred and fifty

acres on the bottom, with three cows and other stock in proportion, and sell butter to those neighbors who have no cows, and to house-boat people.   As for these latter, though they were her customers, she had none too good an opinion of them; they pretended to fish, but in reality only picked up a living from the farmers; nevertheless, she did know of some "weakly, delicate people" who had taken to boat life for economy's sake, and because an invalid could at least fish, and his family help him at it.

NEAR HUNTINGTON, W. VA., Friday, May 18th.—Backed by ravine-grooved hills, and edged at the waterside with great picturesque boulders, planed and polished by the ever-rushing river, the little bottom farms along our path to-day are pretty bits.   But the houses are the reverse of this, having much the aspect of slave-cabins of the olden time—small, one-story, log and frame shanties, roof and gables shingled with "shakes," and little vegetable gardens inclosed by palings.   The majority of these small farmers—whose tracts seldom exceed a hundred acres—rent their land, rather than own it.   The plan seems to be half-and-

half as to crops, with a rental fee for house
and pasturage.   One man, having a hundred-
and-twenty acres, told me he paid three dollars
a month for his house, and for pasturage a
dollar a month per head.

We were in several of the small towns to-
day.   At Millersport, O. (293 miles), while
W— and the Doctor were up town, the Boy
and I remained at the wharf-boat to talk with
the owner.   The wharf-boat is a conspicuous
object at every landing of importance, being a
covered barge used as a storehouse for coming
and going steamboat freight.   It is a private
enterprise, for public convenience, with certain monopolistic privileges at the incorporated
towns.   This Millersport boat cost twelve hundred dollars; the proprietor charges twenty per
cent of each freight-bill, for handling and stor-
ing goods, a fee of twenty-five cents for each
steamer that lands, and certain special fees
for live stock.   Athalia, Haskellville and
Guyandotte were other representative towns.
Stave-making appears to be the chief industry,
and, as timber is getting scarce, the communities show signs of decay.

We had been told, above, that Huntington,
W. Va. (306 miles), was "a right smart chunk

of a town." And it is. There are sixteen
thousand people here, in a finely-built city
spread over a broad, flat plain. Brick and
stone business buildings abound; the broad
streets are paved with brick, and an electric-
car line runs out along the bottom, through
the suburb of Ceredo, W. Va., to Catlettsburg, Ky., nine miles away. Huntington
is the center of a large group of riverside towns
supported by iron-making and other industries—Guyandotte and Ceredo, in West Virginia; Catlettsburg, just over the border in
Kentucky; and Proctorville, Broderickville,
Frampton, Burlington, and South Point, on
the opposite shore.

We are camping to-night in the dense willow grove which lines the West Virginia beach
from Huntington to the Big Sandy. Above
us, on the wide terrace, are fields and orchards,
beyond which we occasionally hear the gong
of electric cars. A public path runs by the
tent, leading from the lower settlements into
Huntington. Among our visitors have been
two houseboat men, whose craft is moored a
quarter of a mile below. One of them is tall,
thick-set, forty, with a round, florid face, and
huge mustaches,—evidently a jolly fellow at

his best, despite a certain dubious, piratical air; a jaunty, narrow-brimmed straw hat is perched over one ear, to add to the general effect; and between his teeth a corn-cob pipe. His younger companion is medium-sized, slim, and loose-jointed, with a baggy gait, his cap thrown over his head, with the visor in the rear—a rustic clown, not yet outgrown his freckles. But three weeks from the parental farm in Putnam County, Ky., the world is as yet a romance to him. The fellow is interesting, because in him can be seen the genesis of a considerable element of the houseboat fraternity. I wonder how long it will be before his partner has him broken in as a river-pirate of the first water.

CHAPTER XII.

IN A FOG—THE BIG SANDY—RAINY WEATH-
ER—OPERATIC GYPSIES—AN ANCIENT TAV-
ERN.

IRONTON, O., Saturday, May 19th.—When
we turned in, last night, it was refreshingly
cool. Heavy clouds were scurrying across the
face of the moon. By midnight, a copious
rain was falling, wind-gusts were flapping our
roof, and a sudden drop in temperature rendered sadly inadequate all the clothing we
could muster into service. We slept late, in
consequence, and, after rigging a wind-break
with the rubber blankets, during breakfast
huddled around the stove which had been
brought in to replace Pilgrim under the fly.
When, at half-past nine, we pushed off, our
houseboat neighbors thrust their heads from
the window and waved us farewell.

A dense fog hung like a cloud over land and
river. There was a stiff north-east wind,
which we avoided by seeking the Ohio shore,

139

where the high hills formed a break; there
too, the current was swift, and carried us
down right merrily.   Shattered by the wind,
great banks of fog rolled up stream, sometimes
enveloping us so as to narrow our view to a
radius of a dozen rods,—again, through the
rifts, giving us momentary glimpses on the
right, of rich green hills, towering dark and
steep above us, iridescent with browns, and
grays, and many shades of green; of whitewashed cabins, single or in groups, standing
out with startling distinctness from som-
bre backgrounds; of houseboats, many-hued,
moored to willowed banks or bolstered high
upon shaly beaches; of the opposite bottom,
with its corrugated cliff of clay; and, now and
then, a slowly-puffing steamboat cautiously
feeling its way through the chilling gloom—a
monster to be avoided by little Pilgrim and her
crew, for the possibility of being run down in
a fog is not pleasant to contemplate.   On
board one of these steamers was a sorry company—apparently a Sunday-school excursion.
Children in gala dress huddled in swarms on
the lee of the great smoke-stacks, and in imagination we heard their teeth chatter as they

glided by us and in another moment were en-
gulfed in the mist.

We catch sight for a moment, through a
cloud crevasse, of Ceredo, the last town in
West Virginia—a small saw-milling community stuck upon the edge of the clay cliff, with
the broad level bottom stretching out behind
like a prairie. A giant railway bridge here
spans the Ohio—a weird, impressive thing, as
we sweep under it in the swirling current, and
crane our necks to see the great stone piers
lose themselves in the cloud. But the Big
Sandy River (315 miles), which divides West
Virginia and Kentucky, was wholly lost to
view. In an opening a few moments later,
however, we had a glimpse of the dark line of
her valley, below which the hills again descend
to the Ohio's bank.

Catlettsburg, the first Kentucky town, is at
the junction, and extends along the foot of
the ridge for a mile or two, apparently not
over two blocks wide, with a few outlying
shanties on the shoulders of the uplands.
Washington was surveying here, on the Big
Sandy, in 1770, and entered for one John Fry
2,084 acres round the site of Louisa, a dozen
miles up the river; this was the first survey

made in Kentucky—but a few months later than Boone's first advent as a hunter on the "dark and bloody ground," and five years before the first permanent settlement in the State. Washington deserves to be remembered as a Kentucky pioneer.

We have not only steamers to avoid, —they appear to be unusually numerous about here, — but snags as well. With care, the whereabouts of a steamer can be distinguished as it steals upon us, from the superior whiteness of its column of "exhaust," penetrating the bank of dark gray fog; and occasionally the echoes are awakened by the burly roar of its whistle, which, in times like this, acts as a fog-horn. But the snag is an insidious enemy, not revealing itself until we are within a rod or two, and then there is a quick cry of warning from the stern sheets—"Hard a-port!" or "Starboard, quick!" and only a strong side-pull, aided by W—'s paddle, sends us free from the jagged, branching mass which might readily have swamped poor Pilgrim had she taken it at full tilt.

At Ashland, Ky. (320 miles), we stopped for supplies. There are six thousand inhabitants here, with some good buildings and a fine, broad, stone wharf, but it is rather a dingy place. The steamer "Bonanza" had just landed. On the double row of flaggings leading up to the summit of the bank, were two ant-like processions of Kentucky folk—one, leisurely climbing townward with their bags and bundles, the other hurrying down with theirs to the boat, which was ringing its bell, blowing off steam, and in other ways creating an uproar which seemed to turn the heads of the negro roustabouts and draymen, who bustled around with a great chatter and much false motion. The railway may be doing the bulk of the business, but it does it unostentatiously; the steamboat makes far more disturbance in the world, and is a finer spectacle. Dozens of boys are lounging at the wharf foot, watching the lively scene with fascinated eyes, probably every one of them stoutly possessed of an ambition akin to that of my young friend in the Cheshire Bottom.

A rain-storm broke the fog—a cold, raw, miserable rain. No clothing we could don appeared to suffice against the chill; and so at last we pitched camp upon the Ohio shore, three miles above the Ironton wharf (325 miles). It is a muddy, dreary nest up here,

among the dripping willows.   Just behind us
on the slope, is the inclined track of the Nor-
folk & Western railway-transfer, down which
trains are slid to a huge slip, and thence ferried
over the river into Kentucky; above that, on a
narrow terrace, is an ordinary railway line; and
still higher, up a slippery clay bank, lies the
cottage-strewn bottom which stretches on into
Ironton (13,000 inhabitants).

We were a sorry-looking party, at lunch this
noon, hovering over the smoking stove which
was set in the tent door, with a wind-screen
in front, and moist bedding hung all about in
the vain hope of drying it in the feeble heat.
And sorrier still, through the long afternoon,
as, each encased in a sleeping-bag, we sat upon
our cots circling around the stove, W— reading to us between chattering teeth from Bar-
rie's *When a Man's Single*. 'Tis good Scot-
tish weather we're having; but somehow our
thoughts could not rest on Thrums, and we
were, for the nonce, a wee bit miserable.

Dinner degenerated into a smoky bite, and
then at dusk there was a council of war.   The
air hangs thick with moisture, our possessions
are in various stages from damp to sopping
wet, and efforts at drying over the little stove

are futile under such conditions.   It was demonstrated that there was not bed-clothing
enough, in such an emergency as this; indeed,
an inspection of that which was merely damp,
revealed the fact that but one person could
be made comfortable to-night.   Our bachelor
Doctor volunteered to be that one.   So we
bade him God-speed, and with toilet bag in
hand I led my little family up a tortuous path,
so slippery in the rain that we were obliged in
our muddy climb to cling to grass-clumps and
bushes.   And thus, wet and bedraggled, did
we sally forth upon the Ironton Bottom, seeking shelter for the night.

Fortunately we had not far to seek.   A
kindly family took us in, despite our gruesome
aspect and our unlikely story—for what manner of folk are we, that go trapesing about in
a skiff, in such weather as this, coming from
nobody knows where and camping o' nights in
the muddy river bottoms?   Instead of sending
us on, in the drenching rain, to a hotel, three
miles down the road, or offering us a ticket on
the Associated Charities, these blessed people
open their hearts and their beds to us, without
question, and what more can weary pilgrims
pray for?

SCIOTOVILLE, O., Sunday, May 20th.—After
breakfast, and settling our modest score, we
rejoined the Doctor, and at ten o'clock pulled
out again; being bidden good-bye at the landing, by the children of our hostess, who had
sent us by them a bottle of fresh milk as a
parting gift.

It had rained almost continuously, throughout the night. To-day we have a dark gray
sky, with fickle winds. A charming color
study, all along our path; the reds and grays
and yellows of the high clay-banks which edge
the reciprocating bottoms, the browns and
yellows of hillside fields, the deep greens of
forest verdure, the vivid white of bankside
cabins, and, in the background of each new
vista, bold headlands veiled in blue. W—
and the Boy are in the stern sheets, wrapped
in blankets, for there is a smart chill in the air,
and we at the oars pull lively for warmth. In
our twisting course, sometimes we have a
favoring breeze, and the Doctor rears the sail;
but it is a brief delight, for the next turn brings
the wind in our teeth, and we set to the blades
with renewed energy. In the main, we make
good time. The sugar-loaf hills, with their

castellated escarpments, go marching by with
stately sweep.

Greenup Court House (334 miles) is a bright
little Kentucky county-seat, well-built at the
feet of thickly-forested uplands.   At the lower
end of the village, the Little Sandy enters
through a wooded dale, which near the mouth
opens into a broad meadow.   Not many miles
below, is a high sloping beach, picturesquely
bestrewn with gigantic boulders which have in
ages past rolled down from the hill-tops above.
Here, among the rocks, we again set up a rude
screen from the still piercing wind; and, each
wrapped in a gay blanket, lunch as operatic
gypsies might, in a romantic glen, enjoying
mightily our steaming chocolate, and the
warmth of our friendly stove—for dessert,
taking a merry scamper for flowers, over the
ragged ascent from whence the boulders came.
Everywhere about is the trumpet creeper, but
not yet in bloom.   The Indian turnip is in
blossom here, and so the smaller Solomon's
seal, yellow spikes of toad-flax, blue and pink
phlox, glossy May apple; high up on the hillside, the fire pink and wintergreen; and, down
by the sandy shore, great beds of blue wild

lupin, and occasionally stately spikes of the familiar moth mullein.

With the temperature falling rapidly, and a drizzling rain taking the starch out of our enthusiasm, we early sought a camping ground. For miles along here, springs ooze from the base of the high clay bank walling in the wide and rocky Ohio beach, and dry spots are few and far between. We found one, however, a half mile above Little Scioto River (346 miles),* with drift-wood enough to furnish us for years, and the beach thick-strewn with fossils of a considerable variety of small bivalves, which latter greatly delighted the Doctor and the Boy, who have brought enough specimens to the tent door to stock a college museum.

Dinner over, the crew hauled Pilgrim under cover, and within prepared for her sailing-master a cosy bed, with the entire ship's stock of sleeping-bags and blankets. W—, the Boy, and I then started off to find quarters in Sciotoville (1,000 inhabitants), which lies just below the river's mouth, here a dozen rods

---

*Two miles up the Little Scioto, Pine Creek enters Perhaps a mile and a half up this creek was, in 1771, a Mingo town called Horse Head Bottom, which cuts some figure in border history as a nest of Indian marauders.

wide.   Scrambling up the slimy bank, through
a maze of thorn trees, brambles, and sycamore
scrubs, we gained the fertile bottom above, all
luscious with tall grasses bespangled with wild
red roses and the showy pentstemon.   The
country road leading into the village is some
distance inland, but at last we found it just
beyond a patch of Indian corn waist high, and
followed it, through a covered bridge, and
down to a little hotel at the lower end of town.

A quaint, old-fashioned house, the Sciotoville tavern, with an inner gallery looking out
into a small garden of peaches, apples, pears,
plums, and grapes—a famous grape country
this, by the way.   In our room, opening from
the gallery, is an antique high-post bedstead;
everywhere about are similar relics of an early
day.   In keeping with the air of serene old
age, which pervades the hostelry, is the white-
haired landlady herself.   In well-starched
apron, white cap, and gold-rimmed glasses,
she benignly sits rocking by the office stove,
her feet on the fender, reading Wallace's
Prince of India; and looking, for all the world,
as if she had just stepped out of some old
portrait of—well, of a tavern-keeping Martha
Washington.

CHAPTER XIII.

Rome, O., Monday, May 21st.—At intervals through the night, rain fell, and the temperature was but 46° at sunrise. However, by the time we were afloat, the sun was fitfully gleaming through masses of gray cloud, for a time giving promise of a warmer day. Dark shadows rested on the romantic ravines, and on the deep hollows of the hills; but elsewhere over this gentle landscape of wooded amphitheatres, broad green meadows, rocky escarpments, and many-colored fields, light and shade gayly chased each other. Never were the vistas of the widening river more beautiful than to-day.

There are saw-mill and fire-brick industries in the little towns, which would be shabby enough in the full glare of day. But they are all glorified in this changing light, which

150

brings out the rich yellows and reds in sharp
relief against the gloomy background of the
hills, and mellows into loveliness the soft
grays of unpainted wood.

At the mouth of the Scioto (354 miles), is
Portsmouth, O. (15,000 inhabitants), a well-
built, substantial town, with good shops. It lies
on a hill-backed terrace some forty feet above
the level of the neighboring bottoms, which
give evidence of being victims of the high
floods periodically covering the low lands
about the junction of the rivers. Just across
the Scioto is Alexandria, and on the Kentucky
side of the Ohio can be seen the white hamlet
of Springville, at the feet of the dentated hills
which here closely approach the river.

The country about the mouth of the Scioto
has long figured in Western annals. Being a
favorite rendezvous for the Shawanese, it naturally became a resort for French and English fur-traders. The principal part of the
first Shawanese village—Shannoah Town, in
the old journals—was below the Scioto's
mouth, on the site of Alexandria; it was the
chief town of this considerable tribe, and here
Gist was warned back, when in March, 1751,
he ventured thus far while inspecting lands for

the Ohio Company. Two years later, there
was a great—perhaps an unprecedented—flood
in the Ohio, the water rising fifty feet above
the ordinary level, and destroying the larger
part of the Shawanese village. Some of the
Indians moved to the Little Miami, and others
up the Scioto, where they built, successively,
Old and New Chillicothe; but the majority
remained, and rebuilt their town on the higher
land north of the Scioto, where Portsmouth
now stands. An outlying band had had, from
before Gist's day, a small town across the
Ohio, the site of Springville; and it was here
that George Croghan had his stone trading
house, which was doubtless, after the manner
of the times, a frontier fortress. In the
French and Indian war (1758), the Shawanese,
tiring of continual conflict, withdrew from
their Ohio River settlements to Old (or Upper) Chillicothe, and thus closed the once important fur-trade at the mouth of the Scioto.

It was while the Indian town at Portsmouth
was still new (1755), that a party of Shawanese brought here a Mrs. Mary Inglis, whom
they had captured while upon a scalping foray
into Southwestern Virginia. The story of the
remarkable escape of this woman, at Big

Bone Lick, of her long and terrible flight through the wilderness along the southern bank of the Ohio and up the Great Kanawha Valley, and her final return to home and kindred, who viewed her as one delivered from the grave, is one of the most thrilling in Western history.*

Although the Shawanese had removed from their villages on the Ohio, they still lived in new towns in the north, within easy striking distance of the great river; and, until the close of the eighteenth century, were a continual source of alarm to those whose business led them to follow this otherwise inviting highway to the continental interior. Flatboats bearing traders, immigrants, and travelers were frequently waylaid by the savages, who exhausted a fertile ingenuity in luring their victims to an ambuscade ashore; and, when not successful in this, would in narrow channels, or when the current swept the craft near land, subject the voyagers to a fierce fusilade of bullets, against which even stout plank barricades proved of small avail.

* See Shaler's *Kentucky* (Amer. Commonwealth series), Collins's *History of Kentucky*, and Hale's *Trans-Alleghany Pioneers*. Shaler gives the date as 1756; but Hale, a specialist in border annals, makes it 1755.

Vanceburgh, Ky. (375 miles), is a little town at the bottom of a pretty amphitheatre of hills. There was a floating photographer there, as we passed, with a gang-plank run out to the shore, and framed specimens of his work hung along the town side of his ample barge. Men with teams were getting wagon-loads of sand from the beach, for building purposes. And, a mile or two down, a float-ing saw and planing-mill—the "Clipper," which we had seen before, up river—was busied upon logs which were being rolled down the beach from the bank above. There are several such mills upon the river, all seem-ingly occupied with "tramp work," for there is a deal of logging carried on, in a small and careful way, by farmers living on these wooded hills.

Vanceburgh was for the time bathed in sunlight; but, as we continued on our way, a heavy rain-cloud came creeping up over the dark Ohio hills, and, descending, cut off our view, at last lustily pelting us as we sat en-cased in rubber. We had been in our pon-chos most of the day, as much for warmth as for shelter; for there was an all-pervading chill, which the fickle sun, breaking its early

promise, had failed to dissipate. Thus, amid
showers alternating with sunbeams, we proceeded unto Rome (381 miles). An Ohio
village, this Rome, and so fallen from its once
proud estate that its postoffice no longer bears
the name—it is simply "Stout's," if, in these
degenerate days, you would send a letter
hither.

It was smartly raining, when we put in on
the stony beach above Rome. The tent went
up in a hurry, and under it the cargo; but by
the time all was housed the sun gushed out
again, and, stretching a line, we soon had our
bedding hung to dry. It is a charming situation; in this melting atmosphere, we have
perhaps the most striking effects of cloud, hill,
bottom, islands, and glancing river, which
have yet been vouchsafed us.

The Romans, like most rural folk along the
river below Wheeling, chiefly drink cistern
water. Earlier in our pilgrimage, we stoutly
declined to patronize these rain-water reser-
voirs, and I would daily go far afield in search
of a well; but lately, necessity has driven us
to accept the cistern, and often we find it
even preferable to the well, on those rare occasions when the latter can be found at vil-

lages or farm-houses.   But there are cisterns
and cisterns—foul holes like that at Rosebud,
others that are neatness itself, with all manner of grades between.   As for river water,
ever yellow with clay, and thick as to motes,
much of it is used in the country parts.   This
morning, a bevy of negroes came down the
bank from a Kentucky field; and each in turn,
creeping out on a drift log,—for the ground is
usually muddy a few feet up from the water's
edge,—lay flat on his stomach and drank
greedily from the roily mess.

At dusk, there was again a damp chill, and
for the third time we left the Doctor to keep
bachelor's hall upon the beach.   It was raining smartly by the time the tavern was reached,
nearly a mile down the bank.   Our advent
caused a rare scurrying to and fro, for two
commercial ''drummers,'' who were to depart
by the early morning boat, occupied the
''reg'lar spar' room,'' the landlady informed us,
and a bit of a cubby-hole off the back stairs
had to be arranged for us.   Guests are rarities, at the hostelry in Rome.

NEAR RIPLEY, O., Tuesday, May 22nd.—
There was an inch of snow last night, on the

hills about, and a morning Cincinnati paper
records a heavy fall in the Pennsylvania
mountains. The storm is general, and the
river rose two feet over night. When we set
off, in mid-morning, it was raining heavily;
but in less than an hour the clouds broke, and
the rest of the day has been an alternation of
chilling showers and bursts of warm sunshine,
with the same succession of alluring vistas,
over which play broad bands of changing light
and shade, and overhead the storm clouds torn
and tossed in the upper currents.

Our landlord at Rome asserted at breakfast
that Kentucky was fifty years behind the Ohio
side, in improvements of every sort. Thus far,
we have not ourselves noticed differences of
that degree. Doubtless before the late civil
war,—all the ante-bellum travelers agree in
this,—when the blight of slavery was resting
on Virginia and Kentucky, the south shore of
the Ohio was as another country; but to-day,
so far as we can ascertain from a surface view,
the little villages on either side are equally
dingy and woe-begone, and large Southern
towns like Wheeling, Parkersburg, Point
Pleasant, and Maysville are very nearly an
offset to Steubenville, Marietta, Pomeroy,

Ironton, and Portsmouth.   North-shore towns
of wealth and prominence are more numerous
than on the Dixie bank, and are as a rule
larger and somewhat better kept, with the
negro element less conspicuous; but to say
that the difference is anywhere near as marked
as the landlord averred, or as my own previous
reading on the subject led me to expect, is
grossly to exaggerate.

After leaving Manchester, O. (394 miles),
with a beautiful island at its door, there are
spasmodic evidences of the nearness of a
great city market.   A large proportion of the
hills are completely denuded of their timber,
and patched with rectangular fields of green,
brown, and yellow; upon the bottoms there
are frequent truck farms; now and then are
stone quarries upon the banks, with capacious
barges moored in front; and upon one or two
rocky ledges were stone-crushers, getting out
material for concrete pavements.   When we
ask the bargemen, in passing, whither their
loads are destined, the invariable reply is,
"The city"—meaning Cincinnati, still seventy
miles away.

Limestone Creek (405 miles) occupies a large
space in Western story, for so insignificant

a stream. It is now not over a rod in width, and at no season can it be over two or three. One finds it with difficulty along the mill-strewn shore of Maysville, Ky., the modern outgrowth of the Limestone village of pioneer days. Limestone, settled four years before Marietta or Cincinnati, was long Kentucky's chief port of entry on the Ohio; immigrants to the new state, who came down the Ohio, almost invariably booked for this point, thence taking stage to Lexington, and travelers in the early day seldom passed it by unvisited. But years before there was any settlement here, the valley of Limestone Creek, which comes gently down from low-lying hills, was regarded as a convenient doorway into Kentucky. When (1776) George Rogers Clark was coming down the river from Pittsburg, with powder given by Patrick Henry, then governor of Virginia, for the defence of Kentucky settlers from British-incited savages, he was chased by the latter, and, putting into this creek, hastily buried the precious cargo on its banks. From here it was cautiously taken overland to the little forts, by relays of pioneers, through a gauntlet of murderous fire.

About twenty-five miles from Limestone,

too, was another attraction of the early time,—
the great Blue Lick sulphur spring; here, in a
valley surrounded by wooded hills, formerly
congregated great herds of buffalo and deer,
which licked the salty earth, and hunters soon
learned that this was a royal ground for game.
The Battle of the Blue Lick (1782) will ever
be famous in the annals of Kentucky.

The Ohio was a mighty waterway into the
continental interior, in the olden days of Limestone. Its only compeer was the so-called
"Wilderness Road," overland through Cumberland Gap—the successor of "Boone's trail,"
just as Braddock's Road was the outgrowth of
"Nemacolin's path." Until several years after
the Revolutionary War, the country north of
the Ohio was still Indian land, and settlement
was restricted to the region south of the river;
so that practically all West-going roads from
the coast colonies centered either on Fort
Pitt or Redstone, or on Cumberland Gap. On
the out-going trip, the Wilderness Road was
the more toilsome of the two, but it was safer,
for the Ohio's banks were beset with thieving
and often murdering savages. In returning
east, many who had descended the river preferred going overland through the Gap, to

painfully pulling up stream through the shallows, with the danger of Indians many times
greater than when gliding down the deep current.   The distance over the two routes from
Philadelphia, was nearly equal, when the windings of the river were taken into account; but
the Carolinians and the Georgians found
Boone's Wilderness Road the shorter of the
two, in their migrations to the promised land
of "Ol' Kaintuck."   And we should not over-
look the fact, that of much importance was
still a third route, up the James and down the
Great Kanawha; a route whose advantage to
Virginia, Washington early saw, and tried in
vain to have improved by a canal connecting
the two rivers.*

Even before the opening of the Revolution,
the Ohio was the path of a considerable emigration.   We have seen Washington going
down to the Great Kanawha with his surveying party, in 1770, and finding that settlers
were hurrying into the country for a hundred
miles below Fort Pitt.   By the close of the
Revolution, the Ohio was a familiar stream.
Pittsburg, from a small trading hamlet and

* See *ante*, p. 126.

11

fording-place, had grown by 1785 to have a thousand inhabitants, chiefly supported by boat-building and the Kentucky carrying trade; and boat-yards were common up both the Monongahela and the Youghiogheny, for a distance of sixty miles. Nevertheless, it was not until 1792 that there were regular conveniences for carrying passengers and freight down the Ohio; the emigrant or trader, on arrival at Pittsburg or Redstone, had generally to wait until he could either charter a boat or have one built for him, although sometimes he found a chance ''passenger flat'' going down.*
This difficulty in securing river transportation was one of the reasons why the majority chose the Wilderness Road.

''The first thing that strikes a stranger from the Atlantic,'' says Flint (1814), ''is the singular, whimsical, and amusing spectacle of the varieties of water-craft, of all shapes and structures.'' These, Flint, who knew the

---

* Palmer (1817) paid five dollars for his passage from Pittsburg to Cincinnati (465 miles), without food, and fifty cents per hundred pounds for freight to Marietta. Imlay (1792) says the rate in his time from Pittsburg to Limestone was twenty-five cents per hundred. In 1803, Harris paid four dollars-and-a-half per hundred for freight, by wagon from Baltimore to Pittsburg.

river well, separates into seven classes: (1)
"Stately barges," the size of an Atlantic
schooner, with "a raised and outlandish-look-
ing deck;" one of these required a crew of
twenty-five to work it up stream.   (2) Keel-
boats—long, slender, and graceful in form,
carrying from fifteen to thirty tons, easily pro-
pelled over the shallows, and much used in
low water, and in hunting trips to Missouri,
Arkansas, and the Red River country.   (3)
Kentucky flats (or "broad-horns"), "a species
of ark, very nearly resembling a New England
pig-stye;" these were from forty to a hundred
feet in length, fifteen feet in beam, and carried from twenty to seventy tons.   Some of
these flats were not unlike the house-boats of
to-day.   "It is no uncommon spectacle to see
a large family, old and young, servants, cattle,
hogs, horses, sheep, fowls, and animals of all
kinds," all embarked on one such bottom.   (4)
Covered "sleds," ferry-flats, or Alleghany
skiffs, carrying from eight to twelve tons.   (5)
Pirogues, of from two to four tons burthen,
"sometimes hollowed from one big tree, or
the trunks of two trees united, and a plank
rim fitted to the upper part."   (6) Common
skiffs and dug-outs.   (7) "Monstrous anom-

alies," not classifiable, and often whimsical in
design.   To these might be added the ''floating shops or stores, with a small flag out to indicate their character,'' so frequently seen by
Palmer (1817), and thriftily surviving unto this
day, minus the flag. And Hall (1828) speaks of a
flat-bottomed row-boat, ''twelve feet long, with
high sides and roof,'' carrying an aged couple
down the river, they cared not where, so long
as they could find a comfortable home in the
West, for their declining and now childless
years.

The first four classes here enumerated, were
allowed to drift down stream with the current,
being steered by long sweeps hung on pivots.
The average speed was about three miles an
hour, but the distances made were considerable, from the fact that in the earliest days
they were, from fear of Indians, usually kept
on the move through day and night,—the
crew taking turns at the sweeps, that the craft
might not be hung up on shore or entangled
in the numerous snags and sawyers.   In going
up stream, the sweeps served as oars, and in
the shallows long pushing-poles were used.

As for the boatmen who professionally pro-
pelled the keels and flats of the Ohio, they

were a class unto themselves—"half horse, half alligator," a contemporary styled them. Rough fellows, much given to fighting, and drunkenness, and ribaldry, with a genius for coarse drollery and stinging repartee. The river towns suffered sadly at the hands of this lawless, dissolute element. Each boat carried from thirty to forty boatmen, and a number of such boats frequently traveled in company. After the Indian scare was over, they generally stopped over night in the settlements, and the arrival of a squadron was certain to be followed by a disturbance akin to those so familiar a few years ago in our Southwest, when the cowboys would undertake to "paint a town red." The boatmen were reckless of life, limb, and reputation, and were often more numerous than those of the villagers who cared to enforce the laws; while there was always present an element which abetted and throve on the vice of the river-men. The result was that mischief, debauchery, and outrage ran riot, and in the inevitable fights the citizens were generally beaten.

The introduction of steamboats (1814) soon effected a revolution. A steamer could carry ten times as much as a barge, could go five times as fast, and required fewer men; it traveled at night, quickly passing from one port to another, pausing only to discharge or receive cargo; its owners and officers were men of character and responsibility, with much wealth in their charge, and insisted on discipline and correct deportment. The flatboat and the keel-boat were soon laid up to rot on the banks; and the boatmen either became respectable steamboat hands and farmers, or went into the Far West, where wild life was still possible.

Shipment on the river, in the flatboat days, was only during the spring and autumnal floods; although an occasional summer rise, such as we are now getting, would cause a general activity. In the autumn of 1818, Hall reports that three millions of dollars' worth of merchandise were lying on the shores of the Monongahela, waiting for a rise of water to float them to their destination. "The Western merchants were lounging discontentedly about the streets of Pittsburg, or moping idly in its taverns, like the victims of an ague." The steamers did something to alleviate this condition of affairs; but it was not until the coming of railways, to carry goods quickly and cheaply across country to deep-water ports like Wheeling, that permanent relief was felt.

But what of the Maysville of to-day? It extends on both sides of Limestone Creek for about two miles along the Kentucky shore, at no point apparently over five squares wide, and for the most part but two or three; for back of it forested hills rise sharply. There is a variety of industries, the business quarter is substantially built, and there are numerous comfortable homes with pretty lawns.

On the opposite shore is Aberdeen, where Kentucky swains and lasses, who for one reason or another fail to get a license at home, find marriage made easy—a peaceful, pleasant, white village, with trees a-plenty, and romantic hills shutting out the north wind.

We are camped to-night on a picturesque sand-slope, at the foot of a willow-edged bottom, and some seven feet above the river level. We need to perch high, for the storm has been general through the basin, and the Ohio is rising steadily.

CHAPTER XIV.

POINT PLEASANT, O., Wednesday, May
23rd.—The river rose three feet during the
night. Steamers go now at full speed, no
longer fearing the bars; and the swash upon
shore was so violent that I was more than
once awakened, each time to find the water
line creeping nearer and nearer to the tent
door. As we sweep onward to-day, upon an
accelerated current, the fringing willows,
whose roots before the rise were many feet up
the slopes of sand and gravel, are gracefully
dipping their boughs in the rushing flood.
With the rise, come the sweepings of the
beaches—bits of lumber, fallen trees, barrels,
boxes, 'longshore rubbish of every sort; sometimes it hangs in ragged rafts, and we steer
clear of such, for Pilgrim's progress is greater
than that of these unwelcome companions of

the voyage, and we wish no entangling alliances.

Much tobacco is raised on the rounded, gently-sloping hills below Maysville. Away up on the acclivities, in sheltered spots near the fields in which they are to be transplanted, or in fence-corners in the ever-broadening bottoms, we note white patches of thin cloth pinned down over the young plants to protect them from untoward frosts.   There are many tobacco warehouses to be seen along the banks—apparently farmers coöperate in maintaining such; and in front of each, a roadway leads down to the water's edge, indicating a steamboat landing.   On the town wharves are often seen portly barrels,—locally, ''puncheons,''—filled with the weed, awaiting shipment by boat; most of the product goes to Louisville, but there are also large buyers in the smaller Kentucky towns.

Occasionally, to-day, we have seen moored to some rustic landing a great covered barge, quite of the fashion of the golden age of Ohio boating.   At one end, a room is partitioned off to serve as cabin, and the sweeps are operated from the roof.   These are produce-boats, which are laden with coarse vegetables and sometimes live stock, and floated down to Cincinnati or Louisville, and even to St. Louis and New Orleans. In ante-bellum days, produce-boats were common enough, and much money was made by speculative buyers who would dispose of their cargo in the most favorable port, sell the barge, and then return by rail or steamer; just as, in still earlier days, the keel or flatboat owner would sell both freight and vessel on the Lower Mississippi,—or abandon the craft if he could not sell it,—and "hoof it home," as a contemporary chronicler puts it.

Ripley, Levanna (417 miles), Higginsport (421 miles), Chilo (431 miles), Neville (435 miles), and Point Pleasant (442 miles) are the Ohio towns to-day; and Dover (417 miles), Augusta (424 miles), and Foster (435 miles), their rivals on the Kentucky shore. Saw-mills and distilleries are the leading industries, and there are broad paved wharves; but a listless air pervades them all, as if once they basked in the light of better days. Foster is rather the shabbiest of the lot. As I passed through to find the postoffice, at the upper edge of town, where the hills come down to meet the bottom, I saw that half of the

store buildings still intact were closed, many
dwellings and warehouses were in ruins, and
numerous open cellars were grown to grass
and weeds. Few people were in sight, and
they loafing at the corners. The postoffice
occupied a vacated store, evidently not swept
these six months past. The youthful master,
with chair tilted back and his feet on an old
washstand which did duty as office table, was
listlessly whittling a finger-ring from a peach-
stone; but shoving his feet along, he made
room for me to write a postal card which I
had brought for the purpose.

"What is the matter with this town?" I
asked, as I scratched away.

"Daid, I reck'n!" and he blew away the
peach-stone dust which had accumulated in
the folds of his greasy vest.

"Yes, I see it is dead. What killed it?"

"Oh! just gone daid—sort o' nat'ral daith,
I reck'n."

We had a pretty view this morning, three
or four miles below Augusta, from the top of
a tree-denuded Kentucky hill, some two hundred and fifty feet high. Hauling Pilgrim
into the willows, we set out over a low, cultivated bottom, whose edges were being lapped

by the rising river, to the detriment of the
springing corn; then scrambling up the terrace on which the Chesapeake & Ohio railway
runs, we crawled under a barb-wire fence,
and ascended through a pasture, our right of
way contested for a moment by a gigantic
Berkshire boar, which was not easily vanquished. When at last we gained the top, by
dint of clambering over rail-fences and up
steep slopes bestrewn with mulleins and boulders, and over patches of freshly-plowed
hardscrabble, the sight was well worth the
rough climb. The broad Ohio bottom, opposite, was thick-dotted with orchard clumps,
from which rose the white houses and barns
of small tillers. On the generous slopes of
the Kentucky hills, all corrugated with wooded
ravines, were scores of fertile farmsteads,
each with its ample tobacco shed—the better class of farmers on the hilltops, their
buildings often silhouetted against the western
sky, and the meaner sort down low on the
river's bank. Through this pastoral scene,
the broad river winds with noble sweep, until,
both above and below, it loses itself in the
purple mist of the distant hills.

We are now upon the Great Bend of the

Ohio, beginning at Neville (435 miles) and ending at Harris's Landing (519 miles), with North Bend (482 miles) at the apex. The bend is itself a series of convolutions, and our point of view is ever changing, so that we have kaleidoscopic vistas,—and with each new setting, good-humoredly dispute with each other, we at the oars, and the others in the stern-sheets, as to which is the more beautiful, the unfolding or the dissolving view.

Our camp to-night is beside a little hillside torrent on the lower edge of Point Pleasant. We are well up on the rocky slope; an abandoned stone-quarry lies back of us, up the hill a bit; and leading into the village, half a mile away, is a picturesque country road, overhung with sumacs and honey locusts—overtopped on one side by a precipitous pasture, and on the other dropping suddenly to a beach thick-grown to willows, maples, and scrub sycamores.

The Boy and I made an expedition into the town, for milk and water, but were obliged to climb one of the sharpest ascents hereabout, before our search was rewarded. A pretty little farmstead it is, up there on the lofty hill above us, with a wealth of chickens and an ample dairy, and fat fields and woods gently sloping backward into the interior. The good farm-wife was surprised that I was willing to "pack" commodities, so plentiful with her, down so steep a path; but canoeing pilgrims must not falter at trifles such as this.

Point Pleasant is the birthplace of General Grant. Not every hamlet has its hero, hereabout. Everyone we met this evening,— seeing we were strangers, the Boy and I,—told us of this halo which crowns their home.

CINCINNATI, Thursday, May 24th.—During the night there were frequent heavy downpours, during which the swollen torrent by our side roared among its boulders right lustily; and occasionally a heavy farm-wagon crossed the country bridge which spans the ravine just above us, its rumblings echoing in the quarried glen for all the world like distant thunder. Before turning in, each built a cairn upon the beach, at the point which he thought the water might reach by morning. The Boy, more venturesome than the rest, piled his cairn highest up the slope; and when daylight revealed the fact that the river, in its four-feet rise, had crept nearest his goal, there was much juvenile rejoicing.

There is a gray sky, this morning. With a cold headwind on the starboard quarter, we hug the lee of the Ohio shore. The river is well up in the willows now. Crowding Pilgrim as closely as we may, within the narrow belt of unruffled water, our oars are swept by their bending boughs, which lightly tremble on the surface of the flood. The numerous rock-cumbered ravines, coursing down the hills or through the bottom lands, a few days since held but slender streams, or were, the most of them, wholly dry; but now they are brimming with noisy currents all flecked with foam—pretty pictures, these yawning gullies, overhung with cottonwoods and sycamores, with thick undergrowth of green-brier and wild columbine, and the yellow buds of the celandine poppy.

The hills are showing better cultivation, as we approach the great city. The farm-houses are in better style, the market gardens larger, prosperity more evident. Among the pleasing sights are frequent farmsteads at the summits of the slopes, with orchards and vineyards, and gardens and fields, stretching down almost to the river—quite, indeed, on the Ohio side, but in Kentucky flanked at the base by the railway

terrace.   Numerous ferries connect the Kentucky railway stations with the eastern bank;
one, which we saw just above New Richmond,
O. (446 miles), was run by horse power, a
weary nag in a tread-mill above each side-
paddle.   Although Kentucky has the railway,
there is just here apparent a greater degree of
thrift in Ohio—the towns more numerous,
fields and truck-gardens more ample, on the
whole a better class of farm-houses, and frequently, along the country road which closely
skirts the shore, comfortable little broad-bal-
conied inns, dependent on the trade of fishing
and outing parties.

Just below the Newport waterworks are
several coal-barge harbors—mooring-grounds
where barges lie in waiting, until hauled off
by tugs to the storage wharves.   In the rear
of one of these fleets, at the base of a market
garden, we found a sunny nook for lunch—for
here on the Kentucky side the cold wind has
full sweep, and we are glad of shelter when at
rest.   Across the river is a broad, low bottom
given up to market gardeners, who jealously
cultivate down to the water's edge, leaving the
merest fringe of willows to protect their do-
main.   At the foot of this fertile plain, the

Little Miami River (460 miles) pours its muddy
contribution into the Ohio; and beyond this
rises the amphitheater of hills on which Cincinnati (466 miles) is mainly built.   We see
but the outskirts here, for two miles below us
there is a sharp bend in the river, and only a
dark pall of smoke marks where the city lies.
But these outlying slopes are well dotted with
gray and white groups of settlement, separated
by stretches of woodland over which play
changing lights, for cloud masses are sweeping
the Ohio hills while we are still basking in
the sun.

Above us, crowning the Kentucky ascents,
or nestled on their wooded shoulders, are many
beautiful villas, evidently the homes of the
ultra-wealthy.   Close at hand we have the
pleasant chink-chink of caulking hammers, for
barges are built and repaired in this snug harbor.   Now and then a river tug comes, with
noisy bluster of smoke and steam, and amid
much tightening and slackening of rope, and
wild profanity, takes captive a laden barge, —
as a cowboy might a refractory steer in the
midst of a herd,—and hauls it off to be dis-
gorged down stream.   And just as we conclude
our lunch, German women come with hoes to

12

practice the gentle art of horticulture—a characteristic conglomeration, in the heart of our busy West; the millionaire on the hill-top, the tiller on the slope, shipwright on the beach, and grimy Commerce master of the flood.

Setting afloat on a boiling current, thick with driftwood, we soon were coursing between city-lined shores—on the Kentucky side, Newport and Covington, respectively above and below Licking River; and in an hour were making our way through the labyrinth of steamers thickly moored with their noses to land, and cautiously creeping around to a quiet spot at the stern of a giant wharf-boat—no slight task this, with the river "on the jump," and a false move liable to swamp us if we strike an obstruction at full gait.   No doubt we all breathed freer when Pilgrim, too, was beached,—although it be only confessed in the privacy of the log.   With her and her cargo safely stored in the wharf-boat, we sought a hotel, and, regaining our bag of clothing,—shipped ahead of us from McKee's Rocks,—donned urban attire for an inspection of the city.

And a noble city it is, that has grown out of the two block-houses which George Rogers

Clark planted here in 1780, on his raid against
the Indians of Chillicothe. In 1788, John
Cleves Symmes, the first United States judge
of the Northwest Territory, purchased from
Congress a million acres of land, lying on the
Ohio between the two Miami Rivers. Mat-
thias Denman bought from him a square mile
at the eastern end of the grant, "on a most
delightful high bank" opposite the Licking,
and—on a cash valuation for the land, of two
hundred dollars—took in with him as partners
Robert Patterson and John Filson. Filson
was a schoolmaster, had written the first history of Kentucky, and seems to have enjoyed
much local distinction. To him was entrusted
the task of inventing a name for the settlement which the company proposed to plant
here. The outcome was "Losantiville," a
pedagogical hash of Greek, Latin, and French:
L, for Licking; *os*, mouth; *anti*, opposite;
ville, city—Licking-opposite-City, or City-op-
posite-Licking, whichever is preferred. This
was in August. The Fates work quickly, for
in October poor Filson was scalped by the
Indians in the neighborhood of the Big Miami,
before a settler had yet been enticed to Losantiville. But the survivors knew how to

"boom" a town; lots were given away by lottery to intending actual settlers; and in a few months Symmes was able to write that "It populates considerably."

A few weeks previous to the planting of Losantiville, a party of men from Redstone had settled Columbia, at the mouth of the Little Miami, about where the suburb of California now is; and, a few weeks later, a third colony was started by Symmes himself at North Bend, near the Big Miami, at the western extremity of his grant; and this, the judge wished to make the capital of the new Northwest Territory. At first, it was a race between these three colonies. A few miles below North Bend, Fort Finney had been built in 1785-86, hence the Bend had at first the start; but a high flood dampened its prospects, the troops were withdrawn from this neighborhood to Louisville, and in the winter of 1789-90 Fort Washington was built at Losantiville by General Harmar. The neighborhood of the new fortress became, in the ensuing Indian war, the center of the district.

To Losantiville, with its fort, came Arthur St. Clair, the new governor of the Northwest Territory (January, 1790); and, making his headquarters here, laid violent hands on Filson's invention, at once changing the name to Cincinnati, in honor of the Society of the Cincinnati, of which the new official was a prominent member—"so that," Symmes sorrowfully writes, "Losantiville will become extinct." Five years of Indian campaigning followed, the features of which were the crushing defeats of Harmar and St. Clair, and the final victory of Mad Anthony Wayne at Fallen Timbers. It was not until the Treaty of Greenville (1795), the result of Wayne's brilliant dash into the wilderness, that the Revolutionary War may properly be said to have ended in the West.

Those were stirring times on the Ohio, both ashore and afloat; but, amidst them all, Cincinnati grew apace. Ellicott, in 1796, speaks of it as "a very respectable place," and in 1814, Flint found it the only port that could be called a town, from Steubenville to Natchez, a distance of fifteen hundred miles; in 1825 he reports it greatly grown, and crowded with immigrants from Europe and from our own Eastern states. The impetus thus early gained has never lessened, and Cincinnati is to-day one of the best built and most substantial cities in the Union.

CHAPTER XV.

THE STORY OF NORTH BEND—THE "SHAKES"—
DRIFTWOOD—RABBIT HASH—A SIDE-TRIP
TO BIG BONE LICK.

NEAR PETERSBURG, KY., Friday, May
25th.—This morning, an hour before noon, as
we looked upon the river from the top of the
Cincinnati wharf, a wild scene presented itself.
The shore up and down, as far as could be
seen, was densely lined with packets and
freighters; beyond them, the great stream,
here half a mile wide, was rushing past like a
mill-race, and black with all manner of drift,
some of it formed into great rafts from each of
which sprawled a network of huge branches.
Had we been strangers to this offscouring of a
thousand miles of beach, swirling past us at a
six-mile gait, we might well have doubted the
prudence of launching little Pilgrim upon such
a sea. But for two days past, we had been
amidst something of the sort, and knew that
to cautious canoeists it was less dangerous
than it appeared.

A strong head wind, meeting this surging
tide, is lashing it into a white-capped fury.
But lying to with paddle and oars, and dodging
ferries and towing-tugs as best we may, Pilgrim
bears us swiftly past the long line of steamers
at the wharf, past Newport and Covington,
and the insignificant Licking,* and out under
great railway bridges which cobweb the sky.
Soon Cincinnati, shrouded in smoke, has disappeared around the bend, and we are in the
fast-thinning suburbs—homes of beer-gardens
and excursion barges, havens for freight-flats,
and villas of low and high degree.

When we are out here in the swim, the
drift-strewn stream has a more peaceful aspect
than when looked at from the shore.   Instead
of rushing past as if dooming to destruction
everything else afloat, the debris falls behind,
when we row, for our progress is then the
greater.   Dropping our oars, our gruesome
companions on the river pass us slowly, for
they catch less wind than we; and then, so
silent the steady march of all, we seem to be
drifting up-stream, until on glancing at the
shore the hills appear to be swiftly going down

---

* So called from the Big Buffalo Lick, upon its banks.

and the willow fringes up,—until the sight makes us dizzy, and we are content to be at quits with these optical delusions.

We no longer have the beach of gravel or sand, or strip of clay knee-deep in mud. The water, now twelve feet higher than before the rise, has covered all; it is, indeed, swaying the branches of sycamores and willows, and meeting the edges of the corn-fields of venturesome farmers who have cultivated far down, taking the risk of a "June fresh." Often could we, if we wished, row quite within the bulwark of willows, where a week ago we would have ventured to camp.

The Kentucky side, to-day, from Covington out, has been thoroughly rustic, seldom broken by settlement; while Ohio has given us a succession of suburban towns all the way out to North Bend (482 miles), which is a small manufacturing place, lying on a narrow bottom at the base of a convolution of gentle, wooded hills. One sees that Cincinnati has a better and a broader base; North Bend was handicapped by nature, in its early race.

When Ohio came into the Union (1803), it was specified that the boundary between her and Indiana should be a line running due

north from the mouth of the Big Miami. But
the latter, an erratic stream, frequently the
victim of floods, comes wriggling down to the
Ohio through a broad bottom grown thick to
willows, and in times of high water its mouth
is a changeable locality. The boundary monument is planted on the meridian of what was
the mouth, ninety-odd years ago; but to-day
the Miami breaks through an opening in the
quivering line of willow forest, a hundred yards
eastward (487 miles).

Garrison Creek is a modest Kentucky affluent, just above the Miami's mouth. At the
point, a group of rustics sat on a log at the
bank-top, watching us approach. Landing in
search of milk and water, I was taken by one
of them in a lumbersome skiff a short distance
up the creek, and presented to his family.
They are genuine "crackers," of the coarsest
type—tall, lean, sallow, fishy-eyed, with tow-
colored hair, an ungainly gait, barefooted, and
in nondescript clothing all patches and tatters.
The tousle-headed woman, surrounded by her
copies in miniature, keeps the milk neatly, in
an outer dairy, perhaps because of market
requirements; but in the crazy old log-house,
pigs and chickens are free comers, and the

cistern from which they drink is foul. Here in this damp, low pocket of a bottom, annually flooded to the door-sill, in the midst of vegetation of the rankest order, and quite unheedful of the simplest of sanitary laws, these yellow-skinned "crackers" are cradled, wedded, and biered. And there are thousands like unto them, for we are now in the heart of the "shake" country, and shall hear enough of the plague through the remainder of our pilgrimage. As for ourselves, we fear not, for it is not until autumn that danger is imminent, and we are taking due precaution under the Doctor's guidance.

Two miles beyond, is the Indiana town of Lawrenceburg, with the unkempt aspect so common to the small river places; and two miles still farther, on a Kentucky bottom, Petersburg, whose chiefest building, as viewed from the stream, is a huge distillery. On a high sandy terrace, a mile or so below, we pitch our nightly camp. All about are willows, rustling musically in the evening breeze, and, soaring far aloft, the now familiar sycamores. Nearly opposite, in Indiana, the little city of Aurora is sparkling with points of light, strains of dance music reach us over the way, and occasional shouts and gay laughter; while now and then, in the thickening dusk of the long day, we hear skiffs go chucking by from Petersburg way, and the gleeful voices of men and women doubtless being ferried to the ball.

NEAR WARSAW, KY., Saturday, May 26th.— Our first mosquito appeared last night, but he was easily slaughtered. It has been a comfort to be free, thus far, from these pests of camp life. We had prepared for them by laying in a bolt of black tarlatan at Wheeling,—greatly superior this, to ordinary white mosquito bar,—but thus far it has remained in the shopman's wrapper.

The fog this morning was of the heaviest. At 4 o'clock we were awakened by the sharp clanging of a pilot's signal bell, and there, poking her nose in among our willows, a dozen feet from the tent, was the "Big Sandy," one of the St. Louis & Cincinnati packet line. She had evidently lost her bearings in the mist; but with a deal of ringing, and a noisy churning of the water by the reversed paddle-wheel, pulled out and disappeared into the gloom.

The river, still rising, is sweeping down an

ever-increasing body of rubbish.   Islands and
beaches, away back to the Alleghanies on the
main stream, and on thousands of miles of
affluents, are yielding up those vast rafts of
drift-wood and fallen timber, which have continually impressed us on our way with a
sense of the enormous wastage everywhere in
progress—necessary, of course, in view of the
prohibitive cost of transportation.   Nevertheless, one thinks pitifully of the tens of thousands who, in congested districts, each winter
suffer unto death for want of fuel; and here is
this wealth of forest debris, the useless plaything of the river.   But not only wreckage of
this character is borne upon the flood.   The
thievish river has picked up valuable saw-logs
that have run astray, lumber of many sorts,
boxes, barrels—and now and then the body of
a cow or horse that has tumbled to its death
from some treacherous clay-cliff or rocky terrace.   The beaches have been swept clean by
the rushing flood, of whatever lay upon them,
be it good or bad, for the great scavenger ex-
ercises no discretion.

The bulk of the matter now follows the
current in an almost solid raft, as it caroms
from shore to shore.   Having swift water

everywhere at this stage, for the most part we
avoid entangling Pilgrim in the procession,
but row upon the outskirts, interested in the
curious medley, and observant of the many
birds which perch upon the branches of the
floating trees and sing blithely on their way.
The current bears hard upon the Aurora
beach, and townsfolk by scores are out in
skiffs or are standing by the water's edge, engaged with boat-hooks in spearing choice
morsels from the debris rushing by their
door—heaping it upon the shore to dry, or
gathering it in little rafts which they moor
to the bank.   It is a busy scene; the wreckers,
men, women, and children alike, are so engaged in their grab-bag game that they have
no eyes for us; unobserved, we watch them
at close range, and speculate upon their respective chances.

Rabbit Hash, Ky. (502 miles), is a crude
hamlet of a hundred souls, lying nestled in a
green amphitheater.   A horse-power ferry runs
over to the larger village of Rising Sun, its
Indiana neighbor.   There is a small general
store in Rabbit Hash, with postoffice and
paint-shop attachment, and near by a tobacco
warehouse and a blacksmith shop, with a few

cottages scattered at intervals over the bottom. The postmaster, who is also the store-keeper and painter, greeted me with joy, as I deposited with him mail-matter bearing eighteen cents' worth of stamps; for his is one of those offices where the salary is the value of the stamps cancelled. It is not every day that so liberal a patron comes along.

"Jemimi! Bill! but guv'm'nt business 's look'n' up—there'll be some o' th' rest o' us a-want'n' this yere off'c', a'ter nex' 'lection, I reck'n'."

It was the blacksmith, who is also the ferry-man, who thus bantered the delighted post-master,—a broad-faced, big-chested, brown-armed man, with his neck-muscles standing out like cords, and his mild blue eyes dancing with fun, this rustic disciple of Tubal Cain. He sat just without the door, leather apron on, and his red shirt-sleeves rolled up, playing checkers on an upturned soap-box, with a jolly fat farmer from the hill-country, whose broad straw hat was cocked on the back of his bald head. The merry laughter of the two was in-fectious. The half-dozen spectators, small farmers whose teams and saddle-horses were hitched to the postoffice railing, were themselves hilarious over the game; and a saffron-skinned, hollow-cheeked woman in a blue sun-bonnet, and with a market-basket over her arm, stopped for a moment at the threshold to look on, and then passed within the store, her eyes having caught the merriment, although her facial muscles had apparently lost their power of smiling.

Joining the little company, I found that the farmer was a blundering player, but made up in fun what he lacked in science.   I tried to ascertain the origin of the name Rabbit Hash, as applied to the hamlet.   Every one had a different opinion, evidently invented on the spur of the moment, but all " 'lowed" that none but the tobacco agent could tell, and he was off in the country for the day; as for them-selves, they had, they confessed, never thought of it before.   It always had been Rabbit Hash, and like enough would be to the end of time.

We are on the lookout for Big Bone Creek, wishing to make a side trip to the famous Big Bone Lick, but among the many openings through the willows of the Kentucky shore we may well miss it, hence make constant inquiry as we proceed.   There was a houseboat in the mouth of one goodly affluent.   As we hove in sight, a fat woman, whose gunny-sack apron was her chief attire, hurried up the gang-plank and disappeared within.

"Hello, the boat!" one of us hailed.

The woman's fuzzy head appeared at the window.

"What creek is this?"

"Gunpowder, I reck'n!"—in a deep, man-like voice.

"How far below is Big Bone?"

"Jist a piece!"

"How many miles?"

"Two, I reck'n."

Big Bone Creek (512 miles), some fifty or sixty feet wide at the mouth, opens through a willow patch, between pretty, sloping hills. A houseboat lay just within—a favorite situation for them, these creek mouths, for here they are undisturbed by steamer wakes, and the fishing is usually good. The proprietor, a rather distinguished-looking mulatto, despite his old clothes and plantation straw-hat, was sitting in a chair at his cabin door, angling; his white wife was leaning over him lovingly, as we shot into the scene, but at once withdrew inside. This man, with his side-whiskers and fine air, may have been a head-waiter or a dance-fiddler in better days; but his soft, plaintive voice, and hacking cough, bespoke the invalid. He told us what he knew about the creek, which was little enough, as he had but recently come to these parts.

At an ordinary stage in the Ohio, the Big Bone cannot be ascended in a skiff for more than half a mile; now, upon the backset, we are able to proceed for two miles, leaving but another two miles of walking to the Lick itself. The creek curves gracefully around the bases of the sugar-loaf hills of the interior. Under the swaying arch of willows, and of ragged, sprawling sycamores, their bark all patched with green and gray and buff and white, we have charming vistas—the quiet water, thick grown with aquatic plants; the winding banks, bearing green-dragons and many another flower loving damp shade; the frequent rocky pal- isades, oozing with springs; and great blue herons, stretching their long necks in wonder, and then setting off with a stately flight which reminds one of the cranes on Japanese ware. Through the dense fringe of vegetation, we have occasional glimpses of the hillside farms— their sloping fields sprinkled with stones, their often barren pastures, numerous abandoned

13

tracts overgrown with weeds, and blue-grass lush in the meadows. Along the edges of the Creek, and in little pocket bottoms, the varied vegetation has a sub-tropical luxuriance, and in this now close, warm air, there is a rank smell suggestive of malaria.

These bottoms are annually overflowed, so that the crude little farmsteads are on the rising ground—whitewashed cabins, many of them of logs, serve as houses; for stock, there are the veriest shanties, affording practically no shelter; best of all, the rude tobacco-drying sheds, in many of which some of last year's crop can still be seen, hanging on the strips. We are out of the world, here; and barefooted men and boys, who with listless air are fishing from the banks, gaze at us in dull wonder as we thread our tortuous way.

Finally, we learned that we could with profit go no higher. Before us were two miles of what was described as the roughest sort of hill road, and the afternoon sun was powerful; so W— accepted the invitation of a rustic fisherman to rest with his "women folks" in a little cabin up the hill a bit. Seeing her safely housed with the good-natured "cracker" farmwife, the Doctor, the Boy, and I trudged off

toward Big Bone Lick.   The waxy clay of the
roadbed had recently been wetted by a shower;
the walking, consequently, was none of the
best.   But we were repaid with charming
views of hill and vale, a softly-rolling scene
dotted with little gray and brown fields, clumps
of woodland, rail-fenced pastures, and cabins
of the crudest sort—for in the autumn-tide,
the curse of malaria haunts the basin of the
Big Bone, and none but he of fortune spurned
would care here in this beauty-spot to plant
his vine and fig-tree.   Now and then our path
leads us across the winding creek, which in
these upper reaches tumbles noisily over ledges
of jagged rock, above which luxuriant sycamores, and elms, and maples arch gracefully.
At each picturesque fording-place, with its
inevitable watering-pool, are stepping-stones
for foot pilgrims; often a flock of geese are
sailing in the pool, with craned necks and
flapping wings hissing defiance to disturbers
of their sylvan peace.

The travelers we meet are on horseback—
most of them the yellow-skinned, hollow-
cheeked folk, with lack-luster eyes, whom we
note in the cabin doors, or dawdling about
their daily routine.   On nearing the Lick,

two young horsewomen, out of the common,
look interestedly at us, and I stop to inquire
the way, although the village spire is peering
above the tree-tops yonder.   Pretty, buxom,
sweet-faced lassies, these, with soft, pleasant
voices, each with her market-basket over her
arm, going homeward from shopping.   It
would be interesting to know their story—
what it is that brings these daughters of a
brighter world here into this valley of the living death.

Two hundred yards farther, where the road
forks, and the one at the right hand ascends
to the small hamlet of Big Bone Lick, there is
an interesting picture beneath the way-post: a
girl in a blue calico gown, her face deep hidden
in her red sunbonnet, sits upon a chestnut
mount, with a laden market-basket before her;
while by her side, astride a coal-black pony,
which fretfully paws to be on his way, is a
roughly dressed youth, his face shaded by a
broad slouched hat of the cowboy order.
They have evidently met there by appoint-
ment, and are so earnestly conversing—she
with her hand resting lovingly, perhaps dep-
recatingly, upon his bridle-arm, and his free
hand nervously stroking her horse's mane,

while his eyes are far afield—that they do not observe us as we pass; and we are free to weave from the incident any sort of cracker romance which fancy may dictate.

The source of Big Bone Creek is a marshy basin some fifty acres in extent, rimmed with gently-sloping hills, and freely pitted with copious springs of a water strongly sulphurous in taste, with a suggestion of salt. The odor is so powerful as to be all-pervading, a quarter of a mile away, and to be readily detected at twice that distance. This collection of springs constitutes Big Bone Lick, probably the most famous of the many similar licks in Kentucky, Indiana, and Illinois.

The salt licks of the Ohio basin were from the earliest times resorted to in great numbers by wild beasts, and were favorite camping-grounds for Indians, and for white hunters and explorers. This one was first visited by the French as early as 1729, and became famous because of the great quantities of remains of animals which lay all over the marsh, particularly noticeable being the gigantic bones of the extinct mammoth—hence the name adopted by the earliest American hunters, "Big Bone." These monsters had evidently been mired in the swamp, while seeking to lick the salty mud, and died in their tracks. Pioneer chronicles abound in references to the Lick, and we read frequently of hunting-parties using the ribs of the mammoth for tent poles, and sections of the vertebræ as camp stools and tables. But in our own day, there are no surface evidences of this once rich treasure of giant fossils; although occasionally a ''find'' is made by enterprising excavators, — several bones having thus been unearthed only a week ago. They are now on exhibition in the neighboring village, preparatory to being shipped to an Eastern museum.

As we hurried back over the rolling highway, thunder-clouds grandly rose out of the west, and great drops of rain gave us moist warning of the coming storm. W— was watching us from the cabin door, as we made the last turning in the road, and, accompanied by the farm-wife and her two daughters, came tripping down to the landing. She had been entertained in the one down-stairs room, as royally as these honest cracker women-folk knew how; seated in the family rocking-chair, she had heard in those two hours the social gossip of a wide neighborhood; learned, too,

that the cold, wet weather of the last fort-
night had killed turkey-chicks and goslings by
the score; heard of the damage being done to
corn and tobacco, by the prevalent high water;
was told how Bess and Brindle fared, off in
the rocky pasture which yields little else than
mulleins; and how far back Towser had to go,
to claim relationship to a collie.   "And
weren't we really show-people, going down
the river this way, in a skiff? or, if we weren't
show-people, had we an agency for something?
or, were we only in trade?"   It seems a difficult task to make these people on the bottoms
believe that we are skiffing it for pleasure—it
is a sort of pleasure so far removed from their
notions of the fitness of things; and so at last
we have given up trying, and let them think
of our pilgrimage what they will.

The entire family now assembled on the
muddy bank, and bade us a really affectionate
farewell, as if we had been, in this isolated
corner of the world, most welcome guests who
were going all too soon.   In a few strokes
of the oars we were rounding the bend; and
waving our hands at the little knot of watch-
ers, went forth from their lives, doubtless
forever.

The storm soon burst upon us in full fury.
Clad in rubber, we rested under giant trees, or
beneath projecting rock ledges, taking advantage of occasional lulls to push on for a few
rods to some new shelter.   The numerous
little hillside runs which, in our journey up,
were but dry gullies choked with leaves and
boulders, were now brimming with muddy torrents, rushing all foam-flecked and with deaf-
ening roar into the central stream.   At last
the cloud curtain rolled away, the sun gushed
out with fiery rays, the arch of foliage sparkled
with splendor—in meadow and on hillside, the
face of Nature was cleanly beautiful.

At the creek mouth, the distinguished mulatto still was fishing from his chair, and standing by his side was his wife throwing a spoon.
They nodded to us pleasantly, as old friends
returned.   Gliding by their boat, Pilgrim was
soon once more in the full current of the swift-
flowing Ohio.

We are high up to-night, on a little grass
terrace in Kentucky, two miles above Warsaw.
The usual country road lies back of us, a rod
or two, and then a slender field surmounted
by a woodland hill.   Fortune favors us, almost

nightly, with beautiful abiding-places.   In no place could we sleep more comfortably than in our cotton home.

CHAPTER XVI.

NEAR MADISON, IND., Sunday, May 27th.— At supper last night, a houseboat fisherman, going by in his skiff, parted the willows fringing our beach, and offered to sell us some of his wares.   We bought from him a two-pound catfish, which he tethered to a bush overhanging the water, until we were ready to dress it; giving us warning, that meanwhile it would be best to have an eye on our purchase, or the turtles would devour it.   Hungry thieves, these turtles, the fisherman said; you could leave nothing edible in water or on land, unprotected, without constant fear of the reptiles— which reminds me that yesterday the Doctor and the Boy found on the beach a beautiful box tortoise.

Our fish was swimming around finely, at

202

the end of his cord, when the executioner arrived, and when finally hung up in a tree was
safe from the marauders. This morning the
fisherman was around again, hoping to obtain
another dime from the commissariat; but
though we had breakfasted creditably from
the little "cat," we had no thought of stock-
ing our larder with his kind. So the grizzly
man of nets took a fresh chew of tobacco, and
sat a while in his boat, "pass'n' th' time o'
day" with us, punctuating his remarks with
frequent expectorations.

The new Kentucky houseboat law taxes each
craft of this sort seven-and-a-half dollars, he
said: five dollars going to the State, and the
remainder to the collector. There was to be
a patrol boat, "to see that th' fellers done
step to th' cap'n's office an' settle." But the
houseboaters were going to combine and fight
the law on constitutional grounds, for they had
been told that it was clearly an interference
with commerce on a national highway. As
for the houseboaters voting—well, some of
them did, but the most of them didn't. The
Indiana registry law requires a six months'
residence, and in Kentucky it is a full year, so
that a houseboat man who moves about any,

"jes' isn't in it, sir, thet's all." However, our
visitor was not much disturbed over the practical disfranchisement of his class—it seemed,
rather, to amuse him; he was much more concerned in the new tax, which he thought an
outrageous imposition. In bidding us a cheery
good-bye, he noticed my kodak. "Yees be
one o' them photygraph parties, hey?" and
laughed knowingly, as though he had caught
me in a familiar trick. No child of nature so
simple, in these days, as not to recognize a
kodak.

Warsaw, Ky. (524 miles), just below, has
some bankside evidences of manufacturing, but
on the whole is rather down at the heel. A
contrast this, to Vevay (533 miles), on the
Indiana shore, which, though a small town on
a low-lying bottom, is neat and apparently
prosperous. Vevay was settled in 1803, by
John James Dufour and several associates,
from the District of Vevay, in Switzerland,
who purchased from Congress four square
miles hereabout, and, christening it New Switzerland, sought to establish extensive vineyards
in the heart of this middle West. The Swiss
prospered. The colony has had sufficient vi-
tality to preserve many of its original charac-

teristics unto the present day.   Much of the
land in the neighborhood is still owned by the
descendants of Dufour and his fellows, but the
vineyards are not much in evidence.   In fact,
the grape-growing industry on the banks of
the Ohio, although commenced at different
points with great promise, by French, Swiss,
Germans, and Americans alike, has not realized their expectations.   The Ohio has proved
to be unlike the Rhine in this respect.   In the
long run, the vine in America appears to fare
better in a more northern latitude.

Three miles above Vevay, near Plum Creek,
I was interested in the Indiana farm upon
which Heathcoat Picket settled in 1795—some
say in 1790.   In his day, Picket was a notable
flatboat pilot.   He was credited with having
conducted more craft down the river to New Orleans, than any other man of his time—going
down on the boat, and returning on foot.   It is
said that he made over twenty trips of this character, which is certainly a marvelous record at a
time when there were only Indian trails through
the more than a thousand miles of dense forest
between Vevay and New Orleans, and when a
savage enemy might be expected to lurk behind any tree, ready to slay the rash pale-face.

Picket's must have been a life of continuous adventure, as thrilling as the career of Daniel Boone himself; yet he is now known to but a local antiquarian or two, and one stumbles across him only in foot-notes. The border annals of the West abound with incidents as romantic as any which have been applauded by men. Daniel Boone is not the only hero of the frontier; he is not even the chief hero,— he is but a type, whom an accident of literature has made conspicuous.

The Kentucky River (541 miles) enters at Carrollton, Ky.,—a well-to-do town, with busy-looking wharves upon both streams,— through a wide and rather uninteresting bottom. But, over beyond this, one sees that it has come down through a deep-cut valley, rimmed with dark, rolling hills, which speak eloquently of a diversified landscape along its banks. The Indian Kentucky, a small stream but half-a-dozen rods wide, enters from the north, five miles below—"Injun Kaintuck," it was called by a jovial junk-boat man stationed at the mouth of the tributary. There are, on the Ohio, several examples of this peculiar nomenclature: a river enters from the south, and another affluent coming in from the north,

nearly opposite, will have the same name with
the prefix "Indian." The reason is obvious;
the land north of the Ohio remained Indian
territory many years after Kentucky and Virginia were recognized as white man's country,
hence the convenient distinction—the river
coming in from the north, near the Kentucky,
for instance, became "Indian Kentucky," and
so on through the list.

Houseboats are less frequent, in these
reaches of the river. The towns are fewer
and smaller than above; consequently there
is less demand for fish, or for desultory labor.
Yet we seldom pass a day, in the most rustic
sections, without seeing from half-a-dozen to
a dozen of these craft. Sometimes they are
a few rods up the mouths of tributaries, half
hidden by willows and overhanging sycamores;
or, in picturesque little openings of the willow
fringe along the main shore; or, boldly planted
at the base of some rocky ledge. At the
towns, they are variously situated: in the
water, up the beach a way, or high upon the
bottom, whither some great flood has carried
them in years gone by. Occasionally, when
high and dry upon the land, they have a bit
of vegetable garden about them, rented for a

time from the farmer; but, even with the floaters, chickens are commonly kept, generally in a coop on the roof, connected with the shore by a special gang-plank for the fowls; and the other day, we saw a thrifty houseboater who had several colonies of bees.

There was a rise of only two feet, last night; evidently the flood is nearly at its greatest. We are now twenty feet above the level of ten days ago, and are frequently swirling along over what were then sharp, stony slopes, and brushing the topmost boughs of the lower lines of willows and scrub sycamores. Thus we have a better view of the country; and, approaching closely to the banks, can from our seats at any time pluck blue lupine by the armful. It thrives mightily on these gravelled shores, and so do the bignonia vine, the poison ivy, and the Virginia creeper. The hills are steeper, now, especially in Indiana; many of them, although stony, worked-out, and almost worthless, are still, in patches, cultivated to the very top; but for the most part they are clothed in restful green. Overhead, in the summer haze, turkey-buzzards wheel gracefully, occasionally chased by audacious hawks; and in the woods, we hear the

warble of song-birds.   Shadowy, idle scenes,
these rustic reaches of the lower Ohio, through
which man may dream in Nature's lap, all
regardless of the workaday world.

It was early evening when we passed Madison, Ind. (553 miles), a fairly-prosperous factory town of about twelve thousand souls.
Scores of the inhabitants were out in boats,
collecting driftwood; and upon the wharf was
a great crowd of people, waiting for an excursion boat which was to return them to Louisville, whence they had come for a day's outing.
It was a lifeless, melancholy party, as excursion folk are apt to be at the close of a gala
day, and they wearily stared at us as we paddled past.

Just below, on the Kentucky shore, on my
usual search for milk and water, I landed at a
cluster of rude cottages set in pleasant market
gardens.   While the others drifted by with
Pilgrim, I had a goodly walk before finding
milk, for a cow is considered a luxury among
these small riverside cultivators; the man who
owns one sells milk to his poorer neighbors.
Such a nabob was at last found.   The animal
was called down from the rocky hills, by her
barefooted owner, who, lank and malaria-

14

skinned, leaned wearily against the well-curb, while his wife, also guiltless of hose and shoes, milked into my pail direct from the lean and hungry brindle.

By the time the crew were reunited, storm-clouds, thick and black, were fast rising in the west.   Scudding down shore for a mile, with oars and paddle aiding the swift current, we failed to find a proper camping-place on the muddy bank of the far-stretching bottom. Rain-drops were now pattering on our rubber spreads, and it was evident that a blow was coming; but despite this, we bent to the work with renewed vigor, and shot across to the lee shore of Indiana—finally landing in the midst of a heavy shower, and hurriedly pitching tent on a rocky slope at the base of a vertical bank of clay.   Above us, a government beacon shines brightly through the persistent storm, with the keeper's neat little house and garden a hundred yards away.   In the tree-tops, up a heavily-forested hill beyond, the wind moans right dismally.   In this sheltered nook, we shall be but lulled to sleep with the ceaseless pelting of the rain.

LOUISVILLE, Monday, May 28th.—At midnight, the heavens cleared, with a cold north wind; the early morning atmosphere was nipping, and we were glad of the shelter of the tent during breakfast. The river fell eight inches during the night, and on either bank is a muddy strip, which will rapidly widen as the water goes down.

Below us, twenty rods or so, moored to the boulder-strewn shore, was a shanty-boat. In the bustle of landing, last night, we had not noticed this neighbor, and it was pitch-dark before we had time to get our bearings. I think it is the most dilapidated affair we have seen on the river—the frame of the cabin is out of plumb, old clothes serve for sides and flap loudly in the wind; while two little boys, who peered at us through slits in the airy walls, looked fairly miserable with cold.

The proprietor of the craft came up to visit us, while breakfast was being prepared, and remained until we were ready to depart—a tall, slouchy fellow, clothed in shreds and patches; he was in the prime of life, with a depressed nose set in a battered, though not unpleasant countenance. None of our party had ever before seen such garments on a human being— old bits of flannel, frayed strips of bagging-

stuff, and other curious odds and ends of fab-
rics, in all the primitive colors, the whole
roughly basted together with sack-thread. He
was a philosopher, was this rag-tag-and-bob-
tail of a man, a philosopher with some mother-
wit about him.   For an hour, he sat on his
haunches, crouching over our little stove, and
following with cat-like care W—'s every movement in the culinary art; she felt she was under
the eye of a critic who, though not voicing his
opinions, looked as if he knew a thing or two.

As a conversationist, our visitor was fluent
to a fault.   It required but slight urging to
draw him out.   His history, and that of his
fathers for three generations back, he recited
in much detail.   He himself had, in his best
days, been a sub-contractor in railway con-
struction; but fate had gone against him, and
he had fallen to the low estate of a shanty-
boatman.   His wife had "gone back on him,"
and he was left with two little boys, whom he
proposed to bring up as gentlemen—"yaas,
sir-r, gen'lem'n, yew hear me! ef I *is* only a
shanty-boat feller!"

"I thote I'd come to visit uv ye," he had
said by way of introduction; "ye're frum a
city, ain't yer? Yaas, I jist thote hit. City

folks is a more 'com'dat'n' 'n country folks.
Why? Waal, yew fellers jist go back 'ere in
th' hills away, 'n them thar country folks
they'd hardly answer ye, they're thet selfish-
like. Give me city folks, I say, fer get'n' long
with!"

And then, in a rambling monologue, while
chewing a straw, he discussed humanity in
general, and the professions in particular. "I
ain't got no use fer lawyers—mighty hard show
them fellers has, fer get'n' to heaven. As fer
doctors—waal, they'll hev hard sledd'n, too;
but them fellers has to do piles o' dis'gree'bl'
work, they do; I'd jist rather fish fer a liv'n',
then be a doctor! Still, sir-r, give me an eddi-
cated man every time, says I. Waal, sir-r,
'n' ye hear me, one o' th' richest fellers right
here in Madison, wuz born 'n' riz on a shanty-
boat, 'n' no mistake. He jist done pick up his
eddication from folks pass'n' by, jes' as yew
fellers is a passin', 'n' they might say a few
wuds o' infermation to him. He done git a
fine eddication jes' thet way, 'n' they ain't no
flies on him, these days, when money-gett'n'
is 'roun'. Jes' noth'n' like it, sir-r! Eddication does th' biz!"

An observant man was this philosopher, and

had studied human nature to some purpose. He described the condition of the poor farmers along the river, as being pitiful; they had no money to hire help, and were an odd lot, any-way—the farther back in the hills you get, the worse they are.

He loved to talk about himself and his lowly condition, in contrast with his former glory as a sub-contractor on the railway. When a man was down, he said, he lost all his friends— and, to illustrate this familiar phase of life, told two stories which he had often read in a book that he owned. They were curious, old-fashioned tales of feudal days, evidently writ-ten in a former century,—he did not know the title of the volume,—and he related them in what evidently were the actual words of the author: a curious recitation, in the pedantic literary style of the ancient story-teller, but in the dialect of an Ohio-river ''cracker.'' His greatest ambition, he told us, was to own a floating sawmill; although he carefully inquired about the laws regulating peddlers in our State, and intimated that sometime he might look us up in that capacity, in our Northern home.

As we approach Louisville to-day, the set-tlements somewhat increase in number, al-

though none of the villages are of great size;
and, especially in Kentucky, they are from
ten to twenty miles apart.   The fine hills continue close upon our path until a few miles
above Louisville, when they recede, leaving
on the Kentucky side a broad, flat plain several miles square, for the city's growth.   For
the most part, these stony slopes are well
wooded with elm, buckeye, maple, ash, oak,
locust, hickory, sycamore, cotton-wood, a few
cedars, and here and there a catalpa and a
pawpaw giving a touch of tropical luxuriance
to the hillside forest; while blackberry bushes,
bignonia vines, and poison ivy, are everywhere abundant; otherwise, there is little of
interest to the botanist.   Redbirds, catbirds,
bluebirds, blackbirds, and crows are chattering noisily in the trees, and turkey-buzzards
everywhere swirl and swoop in mid-air.

The narrow little bottoms are sandy; and
on lowland as well as highland there is much
poor, rock-bewitched soil.   The little whitewashed farmsteads look pretty enough in
the morning haze, lying half hid in forest
clumps; but upon approach they invariably
prove unkempt and dirty, and swarming with
shiftless, barefooted, unhealthy folk, whom

no imagination can invest with picturesque qualities. Their ragged, unpainted tobacco-sheds are straggling about, over the hills; and here and there a white patch in the corner of a gray field indicates a nursery of tobacco plants, soon to be transplanted into ampler soil.

It is not uncommon to find upon a hillside a freshly-built log-cabin, set in the midst of a clearing, with bristling stumps all around, re-minding one of the homes of new settlers on the far-away logging-streams of Northern Wisconsin or Minnesota; the resemblance is the closer, for such notches cut in the edge of the Indiana and Kentucky wilderness are often found after a row of many miles through a winding forest solitude apparently but little changed from primeval conditions. Now and then we come across quarries, where stone is slid down great chutes to barges which lie moored by the rocky bank; and frequently is the stream lined with great boulders, which stand knee-deep in the flood that eddies and gurgles around them.

On the upper edge of the great Louisville plain, we pitched tent in the middle of the afternoon; and, having brought our bag of

land-clothes with us in the skiff, from Cincinnati, took turns under the canvas in effecting
what transformation was desirable, preparatory to a visit in the city.   In the early twilight we were floating past Towhead Island,
with its almost solid flank of houseboats,
threading our way through a little fleet of
pleasure yachts, and at last shooting into the
snug harbor of the Boat Club.   The good-
natured captain of the U. S. Life Saving Station took Pilgrim and her cargo in charge for
the night, and by dusk we were bowling over
metropolitan pavements *en route* to the house
of our friend—strange contrast, this lap of
luxury, to the soldier-like simplicity of our
canvas home.   We have been roughing it for
so long,—less than a month, although it seems
a year,—that all these conveniences of civilization, these social conventionalities, have to
us a sort of foreign air.   Thus easily may man
descend into the savage state.

CHAPTER XVII.

SAND ISLAND, Tuesday, May 29th.—Our
Louisville host is the best living authority on
the annals of his town. It was a delight and
an inspiration to go with him, to-day, the
rounds of the historic places. Much that was
to me heretofore foggy in Louisville story was
made clear, upon becoming familiar with the
setting. The contention is made that La
Salle was here at the Falls of the Ohio, during
the closing months of 1669; but it was over a
century later, under British domination, before a settlement was thought of. Dr. John
Connolly entertained a scheme for founding a
town at the Falls, but Lord Dunmore's War
(1774), and the Revolution quickly following,
combined to put an end to it; so that when
George Rogers Clark arrived on the scene with

his little band of Virginian volunteers (May,
1778), en route to capture the Northwest for
the State of Virginia, he found naught but a
savage-haunted wilderness.   His log fort on
Corn Island, in the midst of the rapids, served
as a base of military operations, and was the
nucleus of American settlement, although later
the inhabitants moved to the mainland, and
founded Louisville.

The falls at Louisville are the only considerable obstruction to Ohio-River navigation.
At an average stage, the descent is but twenty-
seven feet in two-and-a-half miles; in high
flood, the rapids degenerate into merely swift
water, without danger to descending craft.
At ordinary height, it was the custom of pioneer boatmen, in descending, to lighten their
craft of at least a third of the cargo, and thus
pass them down to the foot of the north-side
portage (Clarksville, Ind.), which is three-
quarters of a mile in length; going up, lightened
boats were towed against the stream.   With
the advent of larger craft, a canal with locks
became necessary—the Louisville and Portland
Canal of to-day, which is operated by the general government.

The action of the water, hastened by the

destruction of trees whose roots originally
bound the loose soil, has greatly worn the
islands in the rapids. Little is now left of
historic Corn Island, and that little is, at low
water, being blasted and ground into cement
by a mill hard by on the main shore. To-
day, with a flood of nearly twenty feet above
the normal stage of the season, not much of
the island is visible,—clumps of willows and
sycamores, swayed by the rushing current,
giving a general idea of the contour. Goose
Island, although much smaller than in Clark's
day, is a considerable tract of wooded land,
with a rock foundation. Clark was once its
owner, his home being opposite on the Indiana
shore, where he had a fine view of the river,
the rapids, and the several islands. As for
Clarksville, somewhat lower down, and back
from the river a half mile, it is now but a
cluster of dwellings on the outskirts of New
Albany, a manufacturing town which is rapidly absorbing all the neighboring territory.

Feeling obliged to make an early start, we
concluded to pass the night just below the
canal on Sand Island, lying between New
Albany and Louisville's noisy manufacturing
suburb, Portland. An historic spot is this

insular home of ours.   At the treaty of Fort
Charlotte, Cornstalk told Lord Dunmore the
legend familiar among Ohio River savages—
that here, in ages past, occurred the last great
battle between the white and the red Indians.
It is one of the puzzles of the antiquarians,
this tradition that white Indians once lived in
the land, but were swept away by the reds;
Cornstalk had used it to spur his followers to
mighty deeds, it was a precedent which Pon-
tiac dwelt upon when organizing his conspiracy, and King Philip is said to have been
inspired by it.   But this is no place to discuss
the genesis of the tale.   Suffice it, that on
Sand Island have been discovered great quantities of ancient remains.   No doubt, in its
day, it was an over-filled burying-ground.

Noises, far different from the clash of savage arms, are in the air to-night.   Far above
our heads a great iron bridge crosses the Ohio,
some of its piers resting on the island,—a busy
combination thoroughfare for steam and electric railways, for pedestrians and for vehicles,
plying between New Albany and Portland.
The whirr of the trolley, the scream and rumble of locomotives, the rattle of wagons; and
just above the island head, the burly roar of

steamboats signaling the locks,—these are the sounds which are prevalent. Through all this hubbub, electric lamps are flashing, and just now a steamer's search-light swept our island shore, lingering for a moment upon the little camp, doubtless while the pilot satisfied his curiosity. Let us hope that savage warriors never o' nights walk the earth above their graves; for such scenes as this might well cause those whose bones lie here to doubt their senses.

NEAR BRANDENBURG, KY., Wednesday, 30th.—We stopped at New Albany, Ind. (603 miles), this morning, to stock the larder and to forward our shore-clothes by express to Cairo. It is a neat and busy manufacturing town, with an excellent public market. A gala aspect was prevalent, for it is Memorial Day; the shops and principal buildings were gay with bunting, and men in Grand Army uniforms stood in knots at the street corners.

The broad, fertile plain on both sides of the river, upon which Louisville and New Albany are the principal towns, extends for eight or nine miles below the rapids. The first hills to approach the stream are those in Indiana.

Salt River, some ten or twelve rods wide, enters from the south twenty-one miles below
New Albany, between uninteresting high clay
banks, with the lazy-looking little village of
West Point, Ky., occupying a small rise of
ground just below the mouth. The Kentucky
hills come close to the bank, a mile or two
farther down, and then the familiar characteristics of the reaches above Louisville are resumed—hills and bottoms, sparsely settled
with ragged farmsteads, regularly alternating.

At five o'clock we put in at a rocky ledge
on the Indiana side, a mile-and-a-half above
Brandenburg.   Behind us rises a precipitous
hill, tree-clad to the summit.   The Doctor
found up there a new phlox and a pretty pink
stone-crop, to add to our herbarium, while here
as elsewhere the bignonia grows profusely in
every crevice of the rock.   At dark, two ragged and ill-smelling young shanty-boat men,
who are moored hard by, came up to see us,
and by our camp-fire to whittle chips and
drone about hard times.   But at last we tired
of their idle gossip, which had in it no element of the picturesque, and got rid of them
by hinting our desire to turn in.

The towns were few to-day, and small.

Brandenburg, with eight hundred souls, was the largest—a sleepy, ill-paved, shambling place, with apparently nobody engaged in any serious calling; its chief distinction is an architectural monstrosity, which we were told is the court-house. The little white hamlet of New Amsterdam, Ind. (650 miles), looked trim and bright in the midst of a green thicket. Richardson's Landing, Ky., is a disheveled row of old deserted houses, once used by lime-burners, with a great barge wrecked upon the beach. At the small, characterless Indiana village of Leavenworth (658 miles), I sought a traveling photographer, of whom I had been told at Brandenburg. My quest was for a dark-room where I might recharge my exhausted kodak; but the man of plates had packed up his tent and moved on—I would no doubt find him in Alton, Ind., fifteen miles lower down.

We have had stately, eroded hills, and broad, fertile bottoms, hemming us in all day, and marvelous ox-bows in the erratic stream. The hillsides are heavily wooded, sometimes the slopes coming straight down to the stony beach, without intervening terrace; where there are such terraces, they are narrow and rocky, and the homes of shanty-men; but upon the bottoms are whitewashed dwellings of frame or log, tenanted by a better class, who sometimes have goodly orchards and extensive corn-cribs. The villages are generally in the deep-cut notches of the hills, where the interior can be conveniently reached by a wagon-road—a country "rumpled like this," they say, for ten or twelve miles back, and then stretching off into level plains of fertility. Now and then, a deserted cabin on the terraces,—windowless and gaunt,—tells the story of some "cracker" family that malaria had killed off, or that has "pulled up stakes" and gone to seek a better land.

At Leavenworth, the river, which has been flowing northwest for thirty miles, takes a sudden sweep to the southwest, and thenceforward we have a rapid current. However, we need still to ply our blades, for there is a stiff head-wind, with an eager nip in it, to escape which we seek the lee as often as may be, and bask in the undisturbed sunlight. Right glad we were, at luncheon-time, to find a sheltered nook amidst a heap of boulders on the Kentucky shore, and to sit on the sun-warmed sand and drink hot tea by the side of

15

a camp-fire, rejoicing in the kindness of Providence.

There are few houseboats, since leaving Louisville; to-day we have seen but three or four—one of them merrily going up stream, under full sail. Islands, too, are few—the Upper and Lower Blue River, a pretty pair, being the first we have met since Sunday. The water is falling, it now being three or four feet below the stage of a few days since, as can readily be seen from the broad dado of mud left on the leaves of willows and sycamores; while the drift, recently an ever-present feature of the current, is rapidly lodging in the branches of the willows and piling up against the sand-spits; and scrawling snags and bobbing sawyers are catching on the bars, and being held for the next ''fresh.''

There is little life along shore, in these lower waters. There are two lines of ever-widening, willowed beach of rock and sand or mud; above them, perpendicular walls of clay, which edge either rocky terraces backed by grand sweeps of convoluted hills,—sometimes wooded to the top, and sometimes eroded into palisades,—or wide-stretching bottoms given over to small farms or maybe dense tangles of forest.

In the midst of this world of shade, nestle
the whitewashed cabins of the small tillers;
but though they swarm with children, it is not
often that the inhabitants appear by the riverside.   We catch a glimpse of them when
landing on our petty errands, we now and
then see a houseboater at his nets, and in the
villages a few lackadaisical folk are lounging
by the wharf; but as a rule, in these closing
days of our pilgrimage, we glide through what
is almost a solitude.   The imagination has
not to go far afield, to rehabilitate the river
as it appeared to the earliest voyagers.

Late in the afternoon, as usual wishing
water and milk, we put ashore in Indiana,
where a rustic landing indicated a settlement
of some sort, although our view was confined
to a pretty, wooded bank, and an unpainted
warehouse at the top of the path.   It was a
fertile bottom, a half-mile wide, and stretching a mile or two along the river.   Three
neat houses, one of them of logs, constituted
the village, and all about were grain-fields
rippled into waves by the northwest breeze.

The first house, a quarter of a mile inland,
I reached by a country roadway; it proved to
be the postoffice of Point Sandy.   Chickens

clucked around me, a spaniel came fawning
for attention, a tethered cow mooed plain-
tively, but no human being was visible.   At
last I discovered a penciled notice pinned to
the horse-block, to the effect that the postmaster had gone into Alton (five miles distant)
for the day; and should William Askins call
in his absence, the said Askins was to remember that he promised to call yesterday, but
never came; and now would he be kind enough
to come without fail to-morrow before sundown, or the postmaster would be obliged to
write that letter they had spoken about.   It
was quite evident that Askins had not called;
for he surely would not have left that mysterious notice sticking there, for all Point Sandy
to read and gossip over.   It is to be hoped
that there will be no bloodshed over this
affair; across the way, in Kentucky, there
would be no doubt as to the outcome.

I looked at Boss, and wondered whether in
Indiana it were felony to milk another man's
cow in his absence, with no ginger jar at
hand, into which to drop a compensatory
dime.   Then I saw that she was dry, and concluded that to attempt it might be thought a
violation of ethics.   The postmaster's well,

too, proved to be a cistern,—pardon the Hi-
bernicism,—and so I went farther.

The other frame house also turned out to
be deserted, but evidently only for the day,
for the lilac bushes in the front yard were
hung with men's flannel shirts drying in the
sun.   A buck goat came bleating toward me,
with many a flourish of his horns, from which
it was plain to be seen why the family wash
was not spread upon the grass.   From here I
followed a narrow path through a wheat-field,
the grain up to my shoulders, toward the log
dwelling.   A mangy little cur disputed my
right to knock at the door; but, flourishing
my two tin pails at him, he flew yelping to
take refuge in the hen-coop.   To my sum-
mons at the portal, there came no response,
save the mewing of the cat within.   It was
clear that the people of Point Sandy were not
at home, to-day.

I would have retreated to the boat, but,
chancing to glance up at the overhanging hills
which edge in the bottom, saw two men sitting on a boulder in front of a rude log hut on
the brink of a cliff, curiously watching my
movements on the plain.   Thankful, now,
that the postmaster's cow had gone dry, and

that these observant mountaineers had not
had an opportunity to misinterpret my conduct, I at once hurried toward the hill, hopeful that at the top some bovine might be
housed, whose product could lawfully be acquired. But after a long and laborious climb,
over shifting stones and ragged ledges, I was
met with the discouraging information that
the only cow in these parts was Hawkins'
cow, and Hawkins was the postmaster,—
" down yon, whar yew were a-read'n' th' no-
tices on th' hoss-block." Neither had they
any water, up there on the cliff-top—" don' use
very much, stranger; 'n' what we do, we done
git at Smithfield's, in th' log-house down yon,
'n' I reck'n their cistern's done gone dry, anyhow!"

" But what is the matter down there?" I
asked of the old man,—they were father and
son, this lounging pair who thus loftily sat in
judgment on the little world at their feet;
" why are all the folks away from home?"

He looked surprised, and took a fresh chew
while cogitating on my alarming ignorance of
Point Sandy affairs: " Why, ain' ye heared?
I thote ev'ry feller on th' river knew thet
yere—why, ol' Hawkins, his wife's brother's

buried in Alton to-day, 'n' th' neighbors done
gwine t' th' fun'ral.   Whar your shanty-boat
been beached, thet ye ain' heared thet yere?"

As the sun neared the horizon, we tried
other places below, with no better success;
and two miles above Alton, Ind. (673 miles),
struck camp at sundown, without milk for our
coffee—for water, being obliged to settle and
boil the roily element which bears us onward
through the lengthening days.   Were there
no hardships, this would be no pilgrimage
worthy of the name.   We are out, philosophically to take the world as it is; he who is not
content to do so, had best not stir from home.

But our camping-place, to-night, is ideal.
We are upon a narrow, grassy ledge; below
us, the sloping beach astrewn with jagged
rocks; behind us rises steeply a grand hillside
forest, in which lie, mantled with moss and
lichens, and deep buried in undergrowth, boulders as large as a "cracker's" hut; romantic
glens abound, and a little run comes noisily
down a ravine hard by,—it is a witching back-
door, filled with surprises at every turn.
Beeches, elms, maples, lindens, pawpaws,
tulip trees, here attain a monster growth,—
with grape-vines, their fruit now set, hanging

in great festoons from the branches; and all about, are the flowers which thrive best in shady solitudes—wild licorice, a small green-brier, and, although not yet in bloom, the sessile trillium. We are thoroughly isolated; a half-mile above us, faintly gleams a government beacon, and we noticed on landing that three-quarters of a mile below is a small cabin flanking the hill. Naught disturbs our quiet, save the calls of the birds at roosting-time, and now and then the hoarse bellow of a passing packet, with its legacy of boisterous wake.

CHAPTER XVIII.

NEAR TROY, IND., Friday, June 1st.—Below Alton, the hills are not so high as above.
We have, however, the same thoroughly rustic
landscape, the same small farms on the bottoms and wretched cabins on the slopes, the
same frontier-like clearings thick with stumps,
the same shabby little villages, and frequent
ox-bow windings of the generous stream, with
lovely vistas unfolding and dissolving with pano-
ramic regularity. It is not a region where houseboaters flourish—there is but one every ten
miles or so; as for steamboats, we see on an
average one a day, while two or three usually
pass us in the night.

A dry, unpainted little place is Alton, Ind.,
with three down-at-the-heel shops, a tavern, a
saloon, and a few dwellings; there was no

bread obtainable here, for love or money, and we were fain to be content with a bag of crackers from the postoffice grocery. The promised photographer, who appears to be a rapid traveler, was said to have gone on to Concordia, eight miles below.

Deep Water Landing, Ind. (676 miles), is a short row of new, whitewashed houses, with a great board sign displaying the name of the hamlet, doubtless to attract the attention of pilots. A rude little show-case, nailed up beside the door of the house at the head of the landing-path, contains tempting samples of crockery and tinware. Apparently some enterprising soul is trying to grow a town here, on this narrow ledge of clay, with his landing and his shop as a nucleus. But it is an unlikely spot, and I doubt if his "boom" will develop to the corner-lot stage.

Rono, Ind., a mile below, with its limewashed buildings set in a bower of trees, at the base of a bald bluff, is a rather pretty study in gray and green and white. The most notable feature is a little school-house-like Masonic hall set high on a stone foundation, with a steep outer stairway—which gives one an impression that Rono is a victim of floods, and that the brethren occasionally come in boats to lodge-meetings.

Concordia, Ky. (681 miles), rests on the summit of a steep clay bank, from which men were loading a barge with bark. Great piles of blocks, for staves, ornamented the crest of the rise—a considerable industry for these parts, we were told. But the photographer, whom we were chasing, had "taken" every Concordian who wished his services, and moved on to Derby, another Kentucky village, which at last we found, six miles father down the river.

The principal occupation of the people of Derby is getting out timber from the hillside forests, six to ten miles in the interior. Oak, elm, and sycamore railway-ties are the specialty, these being worth twenty cents each when landed upon the wharf. A few months ago, Derby was completely destroyed by fire, but, although the timber business is on the wane here, much of the place was rebuilt on the old foundations; hence the fresh, unpainted buildings, with battlement fronts, which, with the prevalence of open-door saloons and a woodsy swagger on the part of the inhabitants, give the place a breezy, frontier aspect now seldom to be met with this side of the Rockies.

Here at last was the traveling photographer. His tent, flapping loudly in the wind, occupied an empty lot in the heart of the village—a saloon on either side, and a lumberman's boarding house across the way, where the "artist" was at dinner, pending which I waited for him at the door of his canvas gallery.   He evidently seeks to magnify his calling, does this raw youth of the camera, by affecting what he conceives to be the traditional garb of the artistic Bohemian, but which resembles more closely the costume of the minstrel stage—a battered silk hat, surmounting flowing locks glistening with hair-oil; a loose velveteen jacket, over a gay figured vest; and a great brass watch-chain, from which dangle silver coins.   As this grotesque dandy, evidently not long from his native village, came mincing across the road in patent-leather slippers, smoking a cigarette, with one thumb in an arm-hole of his vest, and the other hand twirling an incipient mustache, he was plainly conscious of creating something of a swell in Derby.

It was a crazy little dark-room to which I

was shown—a portable affair, much like a coffin-case, which I expected momentarily to upset as I stood within, and be smothered in a cloud of ill-smelling chemicals.   However, with care I finally emerged without accident, and sufficiently compensated the artist, who seemed not over-favorable to amateur competition, although he chatted freely enough about his business.   It generally took him ten days, he said, to "finish" a town of five or six hundred inhabitants, like Derby.   He traveled on steamers with his tenting outfit, but next season hoped to have money enough to " do the thing in style," in a houseboat of his own, an establishment which would cost say four hundred dollars; then, in the winter, he could beach himself at some fair-sized town, and perhaps make his board by running a local gallery, taking to the water again on the earliest spring "fresh." "I could live like a fight'n' cock then, cap'n, yew jist bet yer bottom dollar!"

The temperature mounted with the progress of the day; and, the wind dying down, the atmosphere was oppressive.   By the time Stephensport, Ky. (695 miles), was reached, in the middle of the afternoon, the sun was

beating fiercely upon the glassy flood, and our
awning came again into play, although it
could not save us from the annoyance of the
reflection.   The barren clay bank at the mouth
of Sinking Creek, upon which lies Stephensport, seemed fairly ablaze with heat, as I went
up into the straggling hamlet to seek for supplies.   There were no eggs to be had here;
but, at last, milk was found in the farther end
of the village, at a modest little cottage quite
embowered in roses, with two century plants
in tubs in the back-yard, and a trim fruit and
vegetable garden to the rear of that, enclosed
in palings.   I remained a few minutes to chat
with the little housewife, who knows her roses
well, and is versed in the gentle art of horticulture.   But her horizon is painfully narrow—first and dearest, the plants about her,
which is not so bad; in a larger way, Stephensport and its petty affairs; but beyond that
very little, and that little vague.

It is ever thus, in such far-away, side-tracked
villages as this—the world lies in the basin of
the hills which these people see from their
doors; if they have something to love and do for,
as this good woman has in her bushes, seeds,
and bulbs, then may they dwell happily in

rustic obscurity; but where, as is more common, the small-beer of neighborhood gossip is their meat and drink, there are no folk on the footstool more wretched than the denizens of a dead little hamlet like Stephensport.

We are housed this night on the Kentucky side, a mile-and-a-half above Cloverport, whose half-dozen lights are glimmering in the stream. In the gloaming, while dinner was being prepared, a ragged but sturdy wanderer came into camp. He was, he said, a mountaineer looking for work on the bottom farms; heretofore he had, when he wanted it, always found it; but this season no one appeared to have any money to expend for labor, and it seemed likely he would be obliged to return home without receiving an offer. We made the stranger no offer of a seat at our humble board, having no desire that he pass the night in our neighborhood; for darkness was coming on apace, and, if he long tarried, the woodland road would be as black as a pocket before he could reach Cloverport, his alleged destination. So starting him off with a biscuit or two, he was soon on his way toward the village, whistling a lively tune.

CROOKED CREEK, IND., Saturday, 2d.—We had but fairly got to bed last night, after our late dinner, when the heavens suddenly darkened, fierce gusts of wind shook the tent violently, and then rain fell in blinding sheets. For a time it was lively work for the Doctor and me, tightening guy-ropes and ditching in the soft sand, for we were in an exposed position, catching the full force of the storm. At last, everything secured, we in serenity slept it out, awakening to find a beautiful morning, the grape-perfumed air as clear as crystal, the outlines of woods and hills and streams standing out with sharp definition, and over all a hushed charm most soothing to the spirit.

Cloverport (705 miles) is a typical Kentucky town, of somewhat less than four thousand inhabitants. The wharf-boat, which runs up and down an iron tramway, according to the height of the flood, was swarming with negroes, watching with keen delight the departure of the "E. D. Rogan," as she noisily backed out into the river and scattered the crowd with great showers of spray from her gigantic stern-wheel. It was a busy scene on board—negro roustabouts shipping the gang-plank, and sing-

ing in a low pitch an old-time plantation mel-
ody; stokers, stripped to the waist, shoveling
coal into the gaping furnaces; chambermaids
hanging the ship's linen out to dry; passengers
crowded by the shore rail, on the main deck;
the bustling mate shouting orders, apparently
for the benefit of landsmen, for no one on
board appeared to heed him; and high up, in
front of the pilot-house, the spruce captain,
in gold-laced cap, and glass in hand, as im-
movable as the Sphinx.

At the head of the slope were a picturesque
medley of colored folk, of true Southern plantation types, so seldom seen north of Dixie.
Two wee picaninnies, drawn in an express
cart by a half-dozen other sable elfs, attracted
our attention, as W— and I went up-town
for our day's marketing.   We stopped to take
a snap-shot at them, to the intense satisfaction of the little kink-haired mother of the
twins, who, barring her blue calico gown,
looked as if she might have just stepped out
of a Zulu group.

Cloverport has brick-works, gas wells, a
flouring-mill, and other industries. The streets
are unkempt, as in most Kentucky towns, and
mules attached to crazy little carts are the

16

chief beasts of burden; but the shops are well-stocked; there were many farmers in town, on horse and mule back, doing their Saturday shopping; and an air of business confidence prevails.

In this district, coal-mines again appear, with their riverside tipples, and their offal defiling the banks. In general, these reaches have many of the aspects of the Monongahela, although the hills are lower, and mining is on a smaller scale. Cannelton, Ind. (717 miles), is the headquarters of the American Cannel Coal Co.; there are, also, woolen and cotton mills, sewer-pipe factories, and potteries. W— and I went up into the town, on an errand for supplies,—we distribute our small patronage, for the sake of frequently going ashore,—and were interested in noting the cheery tone of the business men, who reported that the financial depression, noticeable elsewhere in the Ohio Valley, has practically been unfelt here. Hawesville, Ky., just across the river, has a similarly prosperous look, but we did not row across to inspect it at close range. Tell City, Ind., three miles below, is another flourishing factory town, whose wharf-boat was the scene of much bustle. Four miles still lower down lies the sleepy little Indiana village of Troy, which appears to have profited nothing from having lively neighbors.

From the neighborhood of Derby, the environing hills had, as we proceeded, been lessening in height, although still ruggedly beautiful. A mile or two below Troy, both ranges suddenly roll back into the interior, leaving broad bottoms on either hand, occasionally edged with high clay banks, through which the river has cut its devious way. At other times, these bottoms slope gently to the beach and everywhere are cultivated with such care that often no room is left for the willow fringe, which heretofore has been an ever-present feature of the landscape. Hereafter, to the mouth, we shall for the most part row between parallel walls of clay, with here and there a bankside ledge of rock and shale, and now and then a cragged spur running out to meet the river. We have now entered the great corn and tobacco belt of the Lower Ohio, the region of annual overflow, where the towns seek the highlands, and the bottom farmers erect their few crude buildings on posts, prepared in case of exceptional flood to take to boats.

The prevalent eagerness on the part of

farmers to obtain the utmost from their land made it difficult, this evening, to find a proper camping-place. We finally found a narrow triangle of clay terrace, in Indiana, at the mouth of Crooked Creek (727 miles), where not long since had tarried a houseboater engaged in making rustic furniture. It is a pretty little bit, in a group of big willows and sycamores, and would be comfortable but for the sand-flies, which for the first time give us annoyance. The creek itself, some four rods wide, and overhung with stately trees, winds gracefully through the rich bottom; we have found it a charming water to explore, being able to proceed for nearly a mile through lovely little wide-spreads abounding in lilies and sweet with the odor of grape-blossoms.

Across the river, at Emmerick's Landing,— a little cluster of unpainted cabins,—lies the white barge of a photographer, just such a home as the Derby artist covets. The Ohio is here about half-a-mile wide, but high-pitched voices of people on the opposite bank are plainly heard across the smooth sounding-board; and in the quiet evening air comes to us the "chuck-chuck" of oars nearly a mile away. Following a torrid afternoon, with exasperating headwinds, this cool, fresh atmosphere, in the long twilight, is inspiring.   Overhead is the slender streak of the moon's first quarter, its reflection shimmering in the broad and placid stream rushing noiselessly by us to the sea.   In blissful content we sit upon the bank, and drink in the glories of the night.   The days of our pilgrimage are nearing their end, but our enthusiasm for this *al fresco* life is in no measure abating.   That we might ever thus dream and drift upon the river of life, far from the labored strivings of the world, is our secret wish, to-night.

We had long been sitting thus, having silent communion with our thoughts, when the Boy, his little head resting on W—'s shoulder, broke the spell by murmuring from the fullness of his heart, "Mother, why cannot we keep on doing this, always?"

YELLOWBANK ISLAND, Sunday, June 3d. — Pilgrim still attracts more attention than her passengers.   When we stop at the village wharfs, or grate our keel upon some rustic landing, it is not long before the Doctor, who now always remains with the boat, no matter who goes ashore, is surrounded by an admiring group, who rap Pilgrim on the ribs, try to lift her by the bow, and study her graceful lines with the air of connoisseurs. Barefooted men fishing on the shores, in broad straw hats, and blue jeans, invariably "pass the time o' day" with us as we glide by, crying out as a parting salute, "Ye've a honey skiff, thar!" or, "Right smart skiff, thet yere!"

We have many long, dreary reaches to-day. Clay banks twelve to twenty feet in height, and growing taller as the water recedes, rise sheer on either side. Fringing the top of each is often a row of locusts, whose roots in a feeble way hold the soil; but the river cuts in at the base, wherever the changing current impinges on the shore, and at low water great slices, with a gurgling splash, fall into the stream, which now is of the color of dull gold, from the clay held in solution. Often, ruins of buildings may be seen upon the brink, that have collapsed from this undercut of the fickle flood; and many others, still inhabited, are in dangerous proximity to the edge, only biding their time.

This morning, we passed the Indiana hamlets of Lewisport (731 miles) and Grand View (736 miles), and by noon were at Rockport

(741 miles), a smart little city of three thousand souls, romantically perched upon a great
rock, which on the right bank rises abruptly
from the wide expanse of bottom.   From the
river, there is little to be seen of Rockport
save two wharves,—one above, the other below, the bold cliff which springs sheer for a
hundred feet above the stream,—two angling
roads leading up into the town, a house or
two on the edge of the hill and a huge water-
tower crowning all.

A few miles below, we ran through a narrow channel, a few rods wide, separating an
elongated island from the Indiana shore.   It
much resembles the small tributary streams,
with a lush undergrowth of weeds down to the
water's edge, and arched with monster sycamores, elms, maples and persimmons.   Frequently had we seen skiffs upon the shore,
arranged with stern paddle-wheels, turned by
levers operated by men standing or sitting in
the boat.   But we had seen none in operation
until, shooting down this side channel, we
met such a craft coming up, manned by two
fellows, who seemed to be having a treadmill
task of it; they assured us, however, that
when a man was used to manipulating the

levers he found it easier than rowing, especially in ascending stream.

Yellowbank Island, our camp to-night, lies nearest the Indiana shore, with Owensboro, Ky. (749 miles), just across the way. We have had no more beautiful home on our long pilgrimage than this sandy islet, heavily grown to stately willows. While the others were preparing dinner, I pulled across the rapid current to an Indiana ferry-landing, where there is a row of mean frame cabins, like the negro quarters of a Southern farm, all elevated on posts some four feet above the level. A half-dozen families live there, all of them small tenant farmers, save the ferryman—a strapping, good-natured fellow, who appears to be the nabob of the community.

Several hollow sycamore stumps house sows and their litters; but the only cow in the neighborhood is owned by a young man who, when I came up, was watering some refractory mules at a pump-trough. He paused long enough to summon Boss and milk a half-gallon into my pail, accepting my dime with a degree of thankfulness which was quite unnecessary, considering that it was *quid pro quo*. Tobacco is a more important crop than

corn hereabout, he said; farmers are rather
impatiently waiting for rain, to set out the
young plants.   His only outbuilding is a monster corn-crib, set high on posts—the airy
basement, no better than an open shed, serv-
ing for a stable; during the few weeks of
severe winter weather, horses and cow are
removed to the main floor, and canvas nailed
around the sides to keep out the wind.   Even
this slight protection is not vouchsafed stock
by all planters; the majority of them appear
to provide only rain shelters, and even these
can be of slight avail in a driving storm.

Later, in the failing light, W— and I pulled
together over to the "cracker" settlement,
seeking drinking-water.   A stout young man
was seated on the end of the ferry barge,
talking earnestly with the ferryman's daughter,
a not unattractive girl, but pale and thin, as
these women are apt to be.   Evidently they
are lovers, and not ashamed of it, for they
gave us a friendly smile as we knotted our
painter to the barge-rail, and expressed great
interest in Pilgrim, she being of a pattern new
to them.

We are in a noisy corner of the world.
Over on the Indiana bottom, a squeaky fiddle is

grinding out dance-tunes, hymns and ballads with charming indifference. We thought we detected in a high-pitched "Annie Laurie" the voice of the ferryman's daughter. There seems, too, to be a deal of rowing on the river, evidently Owensboro folk getting back to town from a day in the country, and country folk hieing home after a day in the city. The ferryman is in much demand, judging from the frequent ringing of his bell,—one on either bank, set between two tall posts, with a rope dangling from the arm. At early dusk, the cracked bell of the Owensboro Bethel resounded harshly in our ears, as it advertised an evening service for the floating population; and now the wheezy strains of a melodeon tell us that, although we stayed away, doubtless others have been attracted thither. The sepulchral roars of passing steamers echo along the wooded shore, the night wind rustles the tree-tops, Owensboro dogs are much awake, and the electric lamps of the city throw upon our canvas screen the fantastic shadows of leaves and dancing boughs.

CHAPTER XIX.

FISHERMEN'S TALES—SKIFF NOMENCLATURE—
GREEN RIVER — EVANSVILLE — HENDER-
SON—AUDUBON AND RAFINESQUE—FLOAT-
ING TRADE—THE WABASH.

GREEN RIVER TOWHEAD, Monday, June
4th.—We were shopping in Owensboro, this
morning, soon after seven o'clock. The business quarter was just stirring into life; and
the negroes who were lounging about on every
hand were still drowsy, as if they had passed
the night there, and were reluctant to be up
and doing. There is a pretty court-house in
a green park, the streets are well paved, and
the shops clean and bright, with their wares
mostly under the awnings on the sidewalk, for
people appear to live much out of doors here—
and well they may, with the temperature 73°
at this early hour, and every promise of a
scorching day.

I wonder if a fisherman could, if he tried,
be exact in his statements. One of them,
below Owensboro, who kept us company for

a mile or two down stream, declared that at this stage of the water he made forty and fifty dollars a week, "'n' I reck'n I ote to be contint." A few miles farther on, another complained that when the river was falling, the water was so muddy the fish would not bite; and even in the best of seasons, a fisherman had "a hard pull uv it; hit ain't no business fer a decent man!" The other day, when the river was rising, a Cincinnati follower of the apostle's calling averred that there was no use fishing when the water was coming up. As the variable Ohio is like the ocean tide, ever rising or falling, it would seem that the thousands in this valley who make fishing their livelihood must be playing a losing game.

There are many beautiful islands on these lower reaches of the river. We followed the narrow channel between Little Hurricane and the Kentucky shore, a charming run of two or three miles, with both banks a dense tangle of drift-wood, weeds and vines. Between Three-Mile Island and Indiana, is another interesting cut-short, where the shores are undisturbed by the work of the main stream, and trees and undergrowth come down to the water's edge; the air is quivering with the

songs of birds, and resonant with sweet smells;
while over stumps, and dead and fallen trees,
grape-vines luxuriantly festoon and cluster.
Near the pretty group of French Islands, two
government dredges, with their boarding
barges, were moored to the Kentucky shore—
waiting for coal, we were told, before resum-
ing operations in the planting of a dike.   I
took a snap-shot at the fleet, and heard one
man shout to another, "Bill, did yer notice
they've a photograph gallery aboord?"   They
appear to be a jolly lot, these dredgers, and
inclined to take life easily, in accordance with
the traditions of government employ.

We frequently see skiffs hauled upon the
beach, or moored between two protecting
posts, to prevent their being swamped by
steamer wakes.   The names they bear interest
us, as betokening, perhaps, the proclivities of
their owners.   "Little Joe," "Little Jim,"
"Little Maggie," and like diminutives, are
common here, as upon the towing-tugs and
steam ferries of broader waters—and now and
then we have, by contrast, "Xerxes," "Achil-
les," "Hercules." Sometimes the skiff is named
after its owner's wife or sweetheart, as
"Maggie G.," "Polly H.," or from the rustic

goddesses, ''Pomona,'' '' Flora,'' ''Ceres;'' on
the Kentucky shore, we have noted ''Stone-
wall Jackson,'' and ''Robert E. Lee,'' and
one Ohio boat was labeled '' Little Phil.''
Literature we found represented to-day, by
''Octave Thanet''—the only case on record,
for the Ohio-River ''cracker'' is not greatly
given to books.   Slang claims for its own,
many of these knockabout craft—'' U. Bet,''
''Git Thair,'' '' Go it, Eli,'' ''Whoa, Emma!''
and nondescripts, like ''Two Doves,'' '' Poker
Chip,'' and '' Game Chicken,'' are not infrequent.

In these stately solitudes, towns are far between.   Enterprise, Ind. (755 miles), is an
unpainted village with a dismal view—back
of and around it, wide bottom lands, with
hills in the far distance; up and down the
river, precipitous banks of clay, with willow
fringes on that portion of the shore which is
not being cut by the impinging current.   Scuf-
fletown, Ky. (767 miles), is uninviting.   Newburgh, on the edge of a bluff, across the river
in Indiana, is a ragged little place that has
seen better days; but the backward view of
Newburgh, from below Three-Mile Island,
made a pretty picture, the whites and reds of

the town standing out in sharp relief against the dark background of the hill.

Green River (775 miles), a gentle, rustic stream, enters through the wide bottoms of Kentucky. We had difficulty in finding it in the wilderness of willows—might not have succeeded, indeed, had not the red smoke-stack of a small steamer suddenly appeared above the bushes. Soon, the puffing craft debouched upon the Ohio, and, quickly overtaking us, passed down toward Evansville.

Green River Towhead, two miles below, claimed us for the night. There is a shanty, midway on the island, and at the lower end the landing of a railway-transfer. We have our camp at the upper end, in a bed of spotless white sand, thick grown to dwarf willows. Entangled drift-wood lies about in monster heaps, lodged in depressions of the land, or against stout tree-trunks; a low bar of gravel connects our home with Green River Island, lying close against the Indiana bank; sand-flies freely joined us at dinner, and I hear, as I write, the drone of a solitary mosquito,—the first in many days; while upon the bar, at sunset, a score of turkey-buzzards held silent council, some of them occasionally rising and

wheeling about in mid-air, then slowly light-
ing and stretching their necks, and flapping
their wings most solemnly, before rejoining
the conference.

CYPRESS BEND, Tuesday, 5th.—The temperature had materially fallen during the night,
and the morning opened gray and hazy.
Evansville, Ind. (783 miles), made a charming
Turneresque study, as her steeples and factory
chimneys developed through the mist. It is
a fine, well-built town, of some fifty thousand
inhabitants, with a beautiful little postoffice
in the Gothic style—a refutation, this, of the
well-worn assertion that there are no credit-
able government buildings in our small American cities. A railway bridge here crosses the
Ohio, numerous sawmills line the bank; altogether, there is business bustle, the like of
which we have not seen since leaving Louisville.

Henderson (795 miles) is a substantial Kentucky town of nine thousand souls, with large
tobacco interests, we are told, ranking next
to Louisville in this regard. Through the
morning, the mist had been thickening.
While we were passing beneath the railway
bridge at Henderson, thunder sounded, and

the western sky suddenly blackened.   Pulling
rapidly in to the town shore, shelter was found
beneath the overhanging deck of a deserted
wharf-boat.   We had just completed prepa-
rations with the rubber blankets and ponchos,
when the deluge came.   But the sheltering
deck was not water-tight; soon the rain came
pouring in upon us through the uncaulked
cracks, and we were nearly as badly off in our
close-smelling quarters as in the open.   However, we were a merry party under there, with
the Doctor giving us a touch of "Br'er Rabbit," and the boy relating a fantastic dream
he had had on the Towhead last night; while
I told them the story of Audubon, whose name
will ever be associated with Henderson.

The great naturalist was in business at
Louisville, early in the century; but in 1812,
he failed in this venture, and moved to Henderson, where his neighbors thought him a
trifle daft,—and certainly he was a ne'er-do-
well, wandering around the woods, with hair
hanging down on his shoulders, a far-away
look in his eyes, and communing with the
birds.   In 1818, the botanist Rafinesque, on
the first of his several tramps down the Ohio
valley,—he had a favorite saying, that the

17

only way for a botanist to travel, was to
walk,—stopped over at Henderson to visit this
crazy fellow of whom he had heard. Rafinesque had a hope that Audubon might buy
some of his colored drawings; but when he
saw the wonderful pictures which Audubon
had made, he acknowledged that his own were
inferior—a sore confession for Rafinesque, who
was an egotist of the first water. Audubon
had but humble quarters, for it was hard work
in those days for him to keep the wolf from
the door; nevertheless, he entertained the distinguished traveler, whom he was himself
destined to far eclipse. One night, a bat flew
into Rafinesque's bedroom, and in driving it
out he used his host's fine Cremona as a club,
thus making kindling-wood of it. Two years
later, still steeped in poverty, Audubon left
Henderson. It was 1826 before he became
known to the world of science, when little of
his life was left in which to enjoy the fame at
last awarded him.

We had lunch on Henderson Island, three
miles down, and for warmth walked briskly
about on the strand, among the willow clumps.
It rained again, after we had taken our seats
in the boat, and the head-wind which sprang

up was not unwelcome, for it necessitated a right lively pull to make headway. W— and the Boy, in the stern-sheets, were not uncomfortable when swathed to the chin in the blankets which ordinarily serve us as cushions.

Ten miles below Henderson, was a little fleet of houseboats, lying in a thicket of willows along the Indiana beach. We stopped at one of them, and bought a small catfish for dinner. The fishermen seemed a happy company, in this isolated spot. The women were engaged in household work, but the men were spending the afternoon collected in the cabin of one of their number, who had recently arrived from Green River. While waiting for the fish to be caught in a live-box, I visited with the little band. It was a comfortable room, furnished rather better than the average shore cabin, and the Green River man's family of half-a-dozen were well-kept, pleasant-faced, and polite. Altogether it was a much more respectable houseboat company than any we have yet seen on the river. But the fish-stories which that Green River man tells, with an honest-like, open-eyed sobriety, would do credit to Munchausen.

The rain, at first spasmodic, became at last

persistent. Two miles farther down, at Cypress Bend (806 miles), we ran into an Indiana hill, where on a steep slope of yellow shale, all strewn with rocks, our tent was hurriedly pitched. There was no driving of pegs into this stony base, so we weighted down the canvas with round-heads, and fastened our guys to bushes and boulders as best we might. Huddled around the little stove, under the fly, the crew dined sumptuously *en course*, from canned soup down to strawberries for dessert, — for Evansville is a good market. It is not always, we pilgrims fare thus high—the resources of Rome, Thebes, Bethlehem, Herculaneum, and the other classic towns with which the Ohio's banks are dotted, being none of the best. Some days, we are fortunate to have aught in our larder.

BROWN'S ISLAND, Wednesday, 6th.—This morning's camp-fire was welcome for its warmth. The sky has been clear, but a sharp, cold wind has prevailed throughout the day, quite counteracting the sun's rays; we noticed townsfolk going about in overcoats, their hands in their pockets. In the ox-bow curves, the breeze came in turn from every quarter, some-

times dead ahead and again pushing us swiftly
on.   In seeking the lee shore, Pilgrim pursued
a zigzag course, back and forth between the
States,—now under the brow of towering clay
banks, corrugated by the flood, and honey-
combed by swallows, which in flocks screamed
and circled over our heads; again, closely
brushing the fringe of willows and sycamores
and maples on low-lying shores.   Thus did
we for the most part paddle in placid water,
while above us the wind whistled in the tree-
tops, rustled the blooming elders and the tall
grasses of the plain, and, out in the open river,
caused white-caps to dance right merrily.

We met at intervals to-day, several houseboats, the most of them bearing the inscription
prescribed by the new Kentucky license law,
which is now being enforced, the essential
features of which inscription are the home and
name of the owner, and the date at which
the license expires.   The standard of education among houseboaters is evinced by the
legend borne by a trader's craft which we
boarded near Slim Island: "Lisens exp.rs
Maye the 24 1895."   The young woman in
charge, a slender creature in a brilliant red
calico gown, with blue ribbons at the corsage,

had been but recently married to her lord, who was back in the country stirring up trade. She had few notions of business, and allowed us to put our own prices on such articles as we purchased. The stock was a curious medley—a few staple groceries, bacon and dried beef, candies, crockery, hardware, tobacco, a small line of patent medicines, in which blood-purifiers chiefly prevailed, bitters, ginger beer, and a glass case in which were displayed two or three women's straw hats, gaudily-trimmed. The woman said their custom was, to tie up to some convenient shore and "buy a little stuff o' the farmers, 'n' in that way trade springs up," and thus become known. Two or three weeks would exhaust any neighborhood, whereupon they would move on for a dozen miles or so. Late in the autumn, they select a comfortable beach, and lie by for the winter.

Mt. Vernon, Ind. (819 miles), is on a high, rolling plain, with a rather pretty little court-house set in a park of grass, some good business buildings, and huge flouring-mills, which appear to be the leading industry. Another flouring-mill town, with the addition of the characteristic Kentucky distillery, is Uniontown (833 miles), on the southern shore—a bright, neat little city, backed by smooth, picturesque green hills.

The feature of the day was the entrance, through a dreary stretch of clay banks, of the Wabash River (838 miles), which divides Indiana from Illinois. Three hundred and sixty yards wide at the mouth, about half the width of the Ohio, it is the most important of the latter's northern affluents, and pours into the main stream a swift-rushing body of clear, green water, which at first boldly pushes over to the heavily-willowed Kentucky shore the roily mess of the Ohio, and for several miles exerts a considerable influence in clarification. The Lower Wabash, flowing through a soft clay bottom, runs an erratic course, and its mouth is a variable location, so that the bounds of Illinois and Indiana, hereabout, fluctuate east and west according to the exigencies of the floods. The far-reaching bottom itself, however, is apparently of slight value, giving evidence, in the dreary clumps of dead timber, of being frequently inundated.

An interesting stream is the Wabash, from an historical point of view. La Salle knew of it in 1677, and was planning to prosecute his fur trade over the Maumee and the Wabash; but the Iroquois held the portage, and for nearly forty years thereafter forbade its use by whites. Joliet thought the Wabash the headwaters of what we know as the Lower Ohio, and in his map (1673) styled the latter the Wabash, down to its mouth. Vincennes, an old Wabash town, was one of the posts captured so heroically for the Americans by George Rogers Clark, during the Revolutionary War. In 1814, there was established at New Harmony, also on the Wabash, the communistic seat of the Harmonists, who had moved thither from Pennsylvania, to which, dissatisfied with the West, they returned ten years later.

Numerous islands have to-day beautified the Ohio. Despite their inartistic names, Diamond and Slim are tipped at head and foot with charming banks and willowed sand, and each center is clothed in a luxurious forest, rimmed by a gravelly beach piled high with drift and gnarled roots: the whole, with startling clearness, inversely reflected in the mirrored flood. Wabash Island, opposite the mouth of the great tributary, is an insular woodland several miles in length.

Among the prettiest of these jewels studding our silvery path, is the upmost of the little group known as Brown's Islands, on which we are passing the night. It was an easy landing on the hard sand, and a comfortable carry to a level opening in the willows, where we have a model camp with a great round sycamore block for a table; an Evansville newspaper does duty as a tablecloth, and two logs rolled alongside make seats. Four miles below, the smoke of Shawneetown (848 miles) rises lazily above the dark level line of woods; while across the river, in Kentucky, there is an unbroken forest fringe, without sign of life as far as the eye can reach. A long glistening bar of sand connects our little island home with the Illinois mainland; upon it was being held, in the long twilight, that evening council of turkey-buzzards, which we so often witness when in an island camp. Sand-pipers went fearlessly about among them, bobbing their little tails with nervous vehemence; redbirds trilled their good-nights in the tree-tops; and, daintily wading in the sandy shallows, object lessons in patience, were great blue herons, carefully peering for the prey which never seems to be found.   As night closed in upon us, owls dismally hooted in the mainland woods, buzzards betook themselves to inland roosts, herons winged their stately flight to I know not where, and over on the Kentucky shore could faintly be heard the barking of dogs at the little "cracker" farmsteads hid deep in the lowland forest.

CHAPTER XX.

HALF-MOON BAR, Thursday, June 7th.—A
head-breeze prevailed all day, strong enough
to fan us into a sense of coolness, but leaving
the water as unruffled as a mill-pond; thus did
we seem, in the vivid reflections of the early
morning, to be sailing between double lines of
shore, lovely in their groupings of luxuriant
trees and tangled heaps of vine-clad drift. It
was a hazy, mirage-producing atmosphere, the
river appearing to melt away in space, and
the ever-charming island heads looming un-
supported in mid-air. From the woods, the
piercing note of locusts filled the air as with
the ceaseless rattle of pebbles against innumerable window-panes.

At a distance, Shawneetown appears as if
built upon higher land than the neighboring
bottom; but this proves, on approach, to be
an optical illusion, for the town is walled in by a

levee some thirty feet in height, above the top of which loom its chimneys and spires. Shawnee-town, laid out in 1808, soon became an important post on the Lower Ohio, and indeed ranked with Kaskaskia as one of the principal Illinois towns, although in 1817 it still only contained from thirty to forty log dwellings. During the reign of the Ohio-River bargemen,* it was notorious as the headquarters of the roughest elements in that boisterous class, and frequently the scene of most barbarous outrages—"the odious receptacle," says a chronicler of the time, "of filth and villany."

In those lively days, which lasted with more or less vigor until about 1830,—by which time, steamboats had finally overcome popular prejudice and gained the upper hand in river transportation,—the people of Shawneetown were largely dependent on the trade of the salt works of the neighboring Saline Reserve. The salt-licks—at which in early days the bones of the mammoth were found, as at Big Bone Lick—commenced a few miles below the town, and embraced a district of about ninety thousand acres. While Illinois was

* See Chapter XIII.

still a Territory, these salines were rented by
the United States to individuals, but were
granted to the new State (1818) in perpetuity.
The trade, in time, decreased with the decadence of river traffic; and Shawneetown has
since had but slow growth—it now being a
dreary little place of three thousand inhabitants, with unmistakable evidences of having
long since seen its best days.

The farmers upon the wide bottoms of the
lower reaches now invariably have their dwellings, corn-cribs, and tobacco-sheds set upon
posts, varying from five to ten feet high, according to the surrounding elevation above
the normal river level. At present we are, as
a rule, hemmed in by banks full thirty or forty
feet in height above the present stage. After
a hard climb up the steps which are frequently
found cut into the clay, to facilitate access
to the river, it is with something akin to awe
that we look upon these buildings on stilts,
for they bespeak, in times of great flood, a
rise in the river of between fifty and sixty feet.

Three miles above Saline River, I scrambled
up to photograph a farm-house of this character. In order to get the building within the
field of the camera, it was necessary to mount

a cob-house of loose rails, which did duty as a pig-pen. A young woman of eighteen or twenty years, attired in a dazzling-red calico gown, came out on the front balcony to see the operation; and, for a touch of life, I held her in talk until the picture was taken. She was not at all averse to thus posing, and chatted as familiarly as though we were old friends. The water, my model said, came at least once a year to the main floor of the house, some ten feet above the level of the land, and forty feet above the normal river stage; "every few years" it rose to the eaves of this story-and-a-half dwelling, when the family would embark in boats, hieing off to the back-lying hills, a mile-and-a-half away. An event of this sort seemed quite commonplace to the girl, and not at all to be viewed as a calamity. As in other houses of the bottom farmers of this district, there is no wall-paper, no plaster upon the walls, and little or nothing else to be injured by water. Their few household possessions can readily be packed into a scow, together with the live-stock, and behold the family is ready, if need be, to float away to the ends of the world. As a matter of fact, if they carry food enough with them, and a rainproof tent, their season on the hills is but a prolonged picnic. When the waters sufficiently subside, they float back again to their home; the river mud is scraped out of the rooms, the kitchen-stove rubbed up a bit, and soon everything is again at rights, with a fresh layer of alluvial deposit to fertilize the fields.

Few of these small farmers own the lands they till; from Pittsburg down, the great majority of Ohio River planters are but tenants. The old families that once owned the soil are living in the neighboring towns, or in other parts of the country, and renting out their acres to these cultivators. We were told that the rental fee around Owensboro is usually in kind,—fourteen bushels of good, salable corn being the rate per acre. In "Egypt," as Southern Illinois is called, the average rent is four or five dollars in money, except in years when the water remains long upon the ground, and thus shortens the season; then the fee is correspondingly reduced. The girl · on the balcony averred, that in 1893 it amounted to one-third the value of the average yield.

The numerous huge stilted corn cribs we see are constructed so that wagons can drive up into them, and, after unloading in bins on either side, descend another incline at the far end. Sometimes a portion of the crib is boarded up for a residence, with windows, and a little balcony which does double duty as a porch and a landing-stage for the boats in time of high water. Scattered about on the level are loosely-built sheds of rails, for stock, which practically live *al fresco*, so far as actual storm-shelter goes.

Usually the flooded bottoms are denuded of trees, save perhaps a narrow fringe along the bank, and a few dead trunks scattered here and there; while back, a third or a half-mile from the river, lies a dense line of forest, far beyond which rises the low rim of the basin. But just below Saline River (857 miles), a lazy little stream of a few rods' width, the hills, now perhaps eighty or a hundred feet in height, again approach to the water's edge; and henceforth to the mouth we are to have alternating semi-circular, wooded bottoms and shaly, often palisaded uplands, grown to scrub and vines much in the fashion of some of the middle reaches. A trading-boat was moored just within the Saline, where we stopped for lunch under a clump of sycamores. The owner obtains butter and eggs from the farmers, in exchange for his varied wares, and sells them at a goodly profit to passing steamers, which will always stop when flagged.

Approaching Cave-in-Rock, Ill. (869 miles), the right bank is for several miles an almost continuous palisade of lime stone, thick-studded with black and brown flints. In the breaking down of this escarpment, popularly styled Battery Rocks, numerous caves have been formed, the largest of which gave the place its name. It is a rather low opening into the rock, perhaps two hundred feet deep, and the floor some twenty feet above the present level of the river; in times of flood, it is frequently so filled with water that boats enter, and thousands of silly people have, in two or three generations past, carved or painted their names upon the vaulted roof.* From this large entrance hall, a chimney-like hole in the roof leads to other chambers, said to be imposing and widely ramified—"not unlike a Gothic cathedral," said Ashe, an early English traveler (1806), who appears to have everywhere in these Western wilds sought the marvellous, and

---

* "Scrawled over by that class of aspiring travelers who defile noble monuments with their worthless names."—Irving, in *The Alhambra*.

18

found it.   About 1801, a band of robbers made
these inner recesses their home, and frequently sallied thence to rob passing boats,
and incidentally to murder the crews.   As for
the little hamlet of Cave-in-Rock, nestled in
a break in the palisade, a few hundred yards
below, it was, between 1801 and 1805, the
seat of another species of brigandage—a land
speculation, wherein schemers waxed rich
from the confusion engendered by conflicting
claims of settlers, the outgrowth of carelessly-
phrased Indian treaties and overlapping French
and English patents.   From 1804 to 1810, a
Congressional committee was engaged in
straightening out this weary tangle; and its
decisions, ratified by Congress, are to-day the
foundation of many land-titles in Indiana and
Illinois.

We are in camp to-night upon the Illinois
shore, opposite Half-Moon Bar (872 miles),
and a mile above Hurricane Island.   Towering above us are great sycamores, cypress,
maples, and elms, and all about a dense jungle
of grasses, vines, and monster weeds—the
rank horse-weed being now some ten feet high,
with a stem an inch in diameter; the dead
stalks of last year's growth, in the broad roll-

ing fields to our rear, indicate a possibility of sixteen feet, and an apparent desire to out-rival the corn. Cane-brake, too, is prevalent hereabout, with stalks two inches or more thick. The mulberries are reddening, the Doctor reports on his return with the Boy from a botanizing expedition, and black-caps are turning; while bergamot and vervain are among the plants newly added to the her-barium.

STEWART'S ISLAND, Friday, 8th.—We arose this morning to find the tent as wet from dew and fog as if there had been a shower, and the bushes by the landing were sparkling with great beads of moisture. The bold, black head of Hurricane Island stood out with start-ling distinctness, framed in rolling fog; through a cloud-bank on the horizon, the sun was bursting with the dull glow of burnished cop-per. By the time of starting, the fog had lifted, and the sun swung clear in a steel-blue sky; but there was still a soft haze on land and river, which dreamily closed the ever-changing vistas, and we seemed to float through an enchanted land.

The approach to Elizabethtown, Ill. (877

miles), is picturesque; but of the dry little town of seven hundred souls, with its rocky, undulating streets set in a break in the line of palisades, very little is to be seen from the river. Quarrying for paving-stones appears to be the chief pursuit of the Elizabethans. At Rose Clare, Ill., a string of shanties three miles below, are two idle plants of the Argyle Lead and Fluor-Spar Mining Co. Carrsville, Ky., is another arid, hillside hamlet, with striking escarpments stretching above and below for several miles. Mammoth boulders, a dozen or more feet in height, relics doubtless of once formidable cliffs, here line the riverside. The palisaded hills reappear in Illinois, commencing at Parkinson's Landing, a dreary little settlement on a waste of barren, stony slope flanking the perpendicular wall.

Just above Golconda Island (890 miles), on the Illinois side, we were witness to a "meet" of farmers for a squirrel-hunt, a favorite amusement in these parts. There were five men upon a side, all carrying guns; as we passed, they were shaking hands, preparatory to separating for the battue. Upon the bank above, in a grove of cypress, pawpaw, and sycamore, their horses were standing, unhitched from the poles of the wagons in which they had been driven, and, tied to trees, feeding from boxes set upon the ground. It was pleasant to see that these people, who must lead dreary lives upon the malaria-stricken and flood-washed bottoms, occasionally take a holiday with a spice of rational adventure in it; although there is the probability that this squirrel-hunt may be followed to-night by a roystering at the village tavern, the losing side paying the score.

We reached Stewart's Island (901 miles) at five o'clock, and went into camp upon the landing-beach of hard, white sand, facing Kentucky. The island is two miles long, the owner living in Bird's Point Landing, Ky., just below us—a rather shabby but picturesquely-situated little village, at the base of pretty, wooded hills. A hundred and fifty acres of the island are planted to corn, and the owner's laborers—a white overseer and five blacks—are housed a half-mile above us, in a rude cabin half-hidden in a generous maple grove.

The white man soon came down to the strand, riding his mule, and both drank freely from the muddy river. He was a fairly-intel-

ligent young fellow, and proud of his mount—
no need of lines, he said, for "this yer mule;
ye on'y say 'gee!' and 'haw!' and he done git
thar ev'ry time, sir-r! 'Pears to me, he jist
done think it out to hisself, like a man would.
Hit ain't no use try'n' boss that yere mule,
he's thet ugly when he's sot on 't—but jist pat
him on th' naick and say, ' So thar, Solomon!'
and thar ain't no one knows how to act better
'n he."

As we were at dinner, in the twilight, the
five negroes also came riding down the angling
roadway, in picturesque single file, singing
snatches of camp-meeting songs in that weird
minor key with which we are so familiar in "ju-
bilee" music.   Across the river, a Kentucky
darky, riding a mule along the dusky woodland road at the base of the hills, and evidently
going home from his work in the fields, was singing at the top of his bent, apparently as a stim-
ulus to failing courage.   Our islanders shouted
at him in derision.   The shoreman's replies,
which lacked not for spice, came clear and
sharp across the half-mile of smooth water,
and his tormentors quickly ceased chaffing.
Having all drunk copiously, men and mules
resumed their line of march up the bank, and

disappeared as they came, still chanting the crude melodies of their people.   An hour later, we could hear them at the cabin, singing "John Brown's Body" and other old friends— with the moon, bright and clear in its first quarter, adding a touch of romance to the scene.

CHAPTER XXI.

The Cumberland and the Tennessee—
Stately solitudes — Old Fort Massac—Dead towns in Egypt—The last
camp—Cairo.

Opposite Metropolis, Ill., Saturday, June
9th.—As we were dressing this morning, at
half-past five, the echoes were again awakened
by the vociferous negro on the Kentucky
shore, who was going out to his work again,
as noisy as ever. One of our own black men
walked down the bank, ostensibly to light his
pipe at the breakfast fire, but really to satisfy
a pardonable curiosity regarding us. The
singing brother on the mainland appeared to
amuse him, and he paused to listen, saying,
''Dat yere nigger, he got too loud voice!''
Then, when he had left our camp and regained
the top of the bank, he leaned upon his hoe
and yelled: ''Say, niggah, ober dere! whar
you git dat mule?''

"Who you holl'rin' at, you brack island niggah?" was the quick reply.

"You lan' niggah, you tink you smart!"

"I'se so smart, I done want no liv'n' on island, wi' gang boss, 'n not 'lowed go 'way!"

The tuneful darky had evidently here touched a tender spot, for our man turned back into the field to his work; and the other, kicking the mule into action, trotted off to the tune of "Dar's a meet'n' here, to-night!"

We went up into the field, to see the laborers cultivating corn. The sun was blazing hot, without a breath of air stirring, but the great black fellows seemed to mind it not, chattering away to themselves like magpies, and keeping up their conversation by shouts, when separated from each other at the ends of plow-rows. A natural levee, eight and ten feet high, and studded with large tree-willows, rims in the island farm like the edge of a basin. We were told that this served as a barrier only against the June "fresh," for the regular spring floods invariably swamp the place; but what is left within the bowl, when the outer waters subside, soon leaches through the sandy soil.

After passing the pretty shores of Dog Island, not far below, the bold, dark headland of Cumberland Island soon bursts upon our view.   We follow the narrow eastern channel, in order to greet the Cumberland River (909 miles), which half-way down its island name-sake,—at the woe-begone little village of Smithland, Ky.,—empties a generous flood into the Ohio, The Cumberland, perhaps a quarter-of-a-mile wide, debouches through high clay banks, which might readily be melted in the turbulent cross-currents produced by the mingling of the rivers; but to avoid this, the government engineers have built a wing-dam running out from the foot of the Cumberland, nearly half-way into the main river. This quickly unites the two streams, and the reinforced Ohio is thereafter perceptibly widened.

Tramp steamers are numerous, on these lower reaches.   We have seen perhaps a dozen such to-day, stopping at the farm landings as well as at the crude and infrequent ham-lets,—mere notches of settlement in the wooded lines of shore,—doing a small busi-ness in chance cargoes and in passengers who flag them from the bank.   A sultry atmos-phere has been with us through the day.   The glassy surface of the river has, when not lashed into foam by passing boats, dazzled the eyes most painfully. The hills, from below Stewart's Island, have receded on either side, generally leaving either low, broad, heavily-timbered bottoms, or high clay banks which stretch back wide plains of yellow and gray corn-land—frequently inundated, but highly pro-ductive. Now and then the encroaching river has remained too long in some belt of forest, and we have great clumps of dead trees, which spring aloft in stately picturesqueness, thickly-clad to the limb-tips with Virginia creeper. A bit of shaly hillside occasionally abuts upon the river, though less frequently than above; and often such a spur has lying at its feet a row of half-immersed boulders, delicately car-peted with mosses and with clinging vines.

The Tennessee River (918 miles), the larg-est of the Ohio's tributaries, is, where it enters, about half the width of the latter. Coming down through a broad, forested bottom, with several pretty islands off its mouth, it presents a pleasing picture. Here again the govern-ment has been obliged to put in costly works to stop the ravages of the mingling torrents in the soft alluvial banks. The Ohio, with the united waters of the Cumberland and the Tennessee, henceforth flows majestically to the Mississippi, a full mile wide between her shores.

Paducah (13,000 inhabitants), next to Louisville Kentucky's most important river port, lies on a high plain just below the Tennessee. It is a stirring little city, with the usual large proportion of negroes, and the out-door business life everywhere met with in the South. Saw-mills, iron plants, and ship-yards line the bank; at the wharf are large steamers doing a considerable business up the Cumberland and Tennessee, and between Paducah and Cairo and St. Louis; and there is a considerable ferry business to and from the Illinois suburb of Brooklyn.

Seven miles below the Tennessee, on the Illinois side, we sought relief from the blazing sun within the mouth of Seven Mile Creek, which is cut deep through sloping banks of mud, and overhung by great sprawling sycamores. These always interest us from the generosity of their height and girth, and from their great variety of color-tones, induced by the patchy scaling of the bark—soft grays, buffs, greens, and ivory whites prevailing.

When sufficiently refreshed in this cool bower, we ventured once more into the fierce light of the open river, and two miles below shot into the broader and more inviting Massac Creek (928 miles), just as, of old, George Rogers Clark did with his little flotilla, when *en route* to capture Kaskaskia. Clark, in his Journal written long after the event, said that this creek is a mile above Fort Massac; his memory failed him—as a matter of fact, the steep, low hill of iron-stained gravel and clay, on which the old stronghold was built, is but two hundred yards below.*

The French commander who, in October, 1758, evacuated and burned Fort Duquesne on the approach of the English army under General Forbes, dropped down the Ohio for nearly a thousand miles, and built ''a new fort on a beautiful eminence on the north bank of the river." But there was a fortified post on this hillock at a much earlier date (about 1711), erected as a headquarters for missionaries, and to guard French fur-traders from

* "In the evening of the same day I ran my Boats into a small Creek about one mile above the old Fort Missack; Reposed ourselves for the night, and in the morning took a Rout to the Northwest."—Clark's letter to Mason.

marauding Cherokees; and Pownall's map notes
one here in 1751. This fort of 1758 was but
an enlarged edition of the old. The new
stronghold, with a garrison of a hundred men,
was the last built by the French upon the Ohio,
and it was occupied by them until they evacuated the country in 1763. England does not
appear to have made any attempt to repair
and occupy the works then destroyed by the
French, although urged to do so by her military agents in the West. Had they held Fort
Massac, no doubt Clark's expedition to capture
the Northwest for the Americans might easily
have been nipped in the bud; as it was, the
old fortress was a ruin when he "reposed" on
the banks of the creek at its feet.

When, in 1793-1794, the French agent
Genet was fomenting his scheme for capturing
Louisiana and Florida from Spain, by the aid
of Western filibusters, old Fort Massac was
thought of as a rallying-point and base of supplies; but St. Clair's proclamation of March
24, 1794, ordering General Wayne to restore
and garrison the place, for the purpose of pre-
venting the proposed expedition from passing
down the river, ended the conspiracy, and Genet
left the country. A year later, Spain, who had at

intervals sought to detach the Westerners from the Union, and ally them with her interests beyond the Mississippi, renewed her attempts at corrupting the Kentuckians, and gained to her cause no less a man than George Rogers Clark himself. Among other designs, Fort Massac was to be captured by the adventurers, whom Spain was to supply with the sinews of war. There was much mysterious correspondence between the latter's corruption agent, Thomas Power, and the American General Wilkinson, at Detroit; but finally Power, in disguise, was sent out of the country under guard, by way of Fort Massac, and his escape into Spanish territory practically ended this interesting episode in Western history. The fort was occupied as a military post by our government until the close of the War of 1812-15; what we see to-day, are the ruins of the establishment then abandoned.

No doubt the face of this rugged promontory of gravel has, within a century, suffered much from floods; but the remains of the earthwork on the crest of the cliff, some fifty feet above the present river-stage, are still easily traceable throughout. The fort was about forty yards square, with a bastion at

each corner; there are the remains of an un-
stoned well near the center; the ditch surrounding the earthwork is still some two-and-
a-half or three feet below the surrounding
level, and the breastwork about two feet above
the inner level; no doubt, palisades once surmounted the work, and were relied upon as the
chief protection from assault. The grounds,
a pleasant grassy grove several acres in extent,
are now enclosed by a rail fence, and neatly
maintained as a public park by the little city
of Metropolis, which lies not far below. It
was a commanding view of land and river,
which was enjoyed by the garrison of old Fort
Massac. Up stream, there is a straight stretch
of eleven miles to the mouth of the Tennessee;
both up and down, the shore lines are under
full survey, until they melt away in the distance. No enemy could well surprise the
holders of this key to the Lower Ohio.

Our camp is on the sandy beach opposite
Metropolis, and two hundred yards below the
Kentucky end of the ferry. Behind us lies a
deep forest, with sycamores six and eight feet
in diameter; a country road curving off through
the woods, to the sparse rustic settlement lying
some two miles in the interior—on higher

ground than this wooded bottom, which is annually overflowed. Now and then the blustering little steam-ferry comes across to land Kentucky farm-folk and their mules, going home from a Saturday's shopping in Metropolis. Occasionally a fisherman passes, lagging on his oars to scan us and our quarters; and from one of them, we purchased a fish. As the still, cool night crept on, Metropolis was astir; across the mile of intervening water, darted tremulous shafts of light; we heard voices singing and laughing, a fiddle in its highest notes, the puffing of a stationary engine, and the bay and yelp of countless dogs. Later, a packet swooped down with smothered roar, and threw its electric search-light on the city wharf, revealing a crowd of negroes gathered there, like moths in the radiance of a candle; there were gay shouts, and a mad scampering—we could see it all, as plainly as if in ordinary light it had been but a third of the distance; and then the roustabouts struck up a weird song as they ran out the gangplank, and, laden with boxes and bales, began swarming ashore, like a procession of black ants carrying pupa cases.

19

Mound City Towhead, Sunday, 10th.—
During the night, burglarious pigs would have
raided our larder, but the crash of a falling
kettle wakened us suddenly, as did geese the
ancient Romans. The Doctor and I sallied
forth in our pajamas, with clods of clay in
hand, to send the enemy flying back into the
forest, snorting and squealing with baffled
rage.

We were afloat at half-past seven, under an
unclouded sky, with the sun sharply reflected
from the smooth surface of the river, and the
temperature rapidly mounting.

The Fort Massac ridge extends down stream
as far as Mound City, but soon degenerates
into a ridge of clay varying in height from
twenty-five to fifty feet above the water level.
Upon the low-lying bottom of the Kentucky
shore, is still an interminable dark line of
forest. The settlements are meager, and now
wholly in Illinois: For instance, Joppa (936
miles), a row of a half-dozen unpainted, dilapidated buildings, chiefly stores and abandoned
warehouses, bespeaking a river traffic of the
olden time, that has gone to decay; a hot,
dreary, baking spot, this Joppa, as it lies
sprawling upon the clay ridge, flanked by a

low, wide gravel beach, on which gaunt, bell-ringing cows are wandering, eating the leaves of fallen trees, for lack of better pasturage. Our pilot map, of sixty years ago, records the presence of Wilkinsonville (942 miles), on the site of old Fort Wilkinson of the War of 1812-15, but no one along the banks appears to have ever heard of it; however, after much searching, we found the place for ourselves, on an eminence of fifty feet, with two or three farm-houses as the sole relics of the old establishment. Caledonia (Olmstead P. O.), nine miles down, consists of several large buildings on a hill set well back from the river. Mound City (959 miles),—the "America" of our time-worn map,—in whose outskirts we are camped to-night, is a busy town with furniture factories, lumber mills, ship-yards, and a railway transfer. Below that, stretches the vast extent of swamp and low woodland on which Cairo (967 miles) has with infinite pains been built—like "brave little Holland," holding her own against the floods solely by virtue of her encircling dike.

Houseboats have been few, to-day, and they of the shanty order and generally stranded high upon the beach. One sees now and then, on the Illinois ridge, the cheap log or frame house of a ''cracker,'' the very picture of desolate despair; but on the Kentucky shore are few signs of life, for the bottom lies so low that it is frequently inundated, and settlement ventures no nearer than two or three miles from the riverside. A fisherman comes occasionally into view, upon this wide expanse of wood and water and clay-banks; sometimes we hail him in passing, always getting a respectful answer, but a stare of innocent curiosity.

Our last home upon the Ohio is facing the Kentucky shore, on the cleanly sand-beach of Mound City Towhead, a small island which in times of high water is but a bar. The tent is screened in a willow clump; just below us, on higher ground, sycamores soar heavenward, gayly festooned with vines, hiding from us Mound City and the Illinois mainland. Across the river, a Kentucky negro is singing in the gloaming; but it is over a mile away, and, while the tune is plain, the words are lost. Children's voices, and the bay of hounds, come wafted to us from the northern shore. A steamer's wake rolls along our island strand, dangerously near the camp-fire;

the river is still falling, however, and we no longer fear the encroachments of the flood. The Doctor and I found a secluded nook, where in the moonlight we took our final plunge.

It is sad, this bidding good-bye to the stream which has floated us so merrily for a thousand miles, from the mountains down to the plain. We elders linger long by the last camp-fire, to talk in fond reminiscence of the six weeks afloat; while the Boy no doubt dreams peace-fully of houseboats and fishermen, of gigantic bridges and flashing steel-plants, of coal-mines and oil-wells, of pioneers and Indians, and all that—of six weeks of kaleidoscopic sensations, at an age when the mind is keenly active, and the heart open to impressions which can never be dimmed so long as his little life shall last.

CAIRO, Monday, 11th.—At our island camp, last night, we were but nine miles from the mouth of the Ohio, a distance which could easily have been made before sundown; but we preferred to reach our destination in the morning, the better to arrange for railway transportation, hence our agreeable pause up-on the Towhead.

Before embarking for the last run, this morning, we made a neat heap on the beach, of such of our stores, edible and wearable, as had been requisite to the trip, but were not worth the cost of sending home. Feeling confident that some passing fisherman would soon be tempted ashore to inspect this curious landmark, and yet might be troubled by nice scruples as to the policy of appropriating the find, we conspicuously labeled it: "Abandoned by the owners! The finder is welcome to the lot."

Quickly passing Mound City, now bustling with life, Pilgrim closely skirted the monotonous clay-banks of Illinois, swept rapidly under the monster railway bridge which stalks high above the flood, and loses itself over the tree-tops of the Kentucky bottom, and at a quarter-past eight o'clock was pulled up at Cairo, with the Mississippi in plain sight over there, through the opening in the forest. In another hour or two, she will be housed in a box-car; and we, her crew, having again donned the garb of landsmen, will be speeding toward our northern home, this pilgrimage but a memory.

Such a memory! As we dropped below the

Towhead, the Boy, for once silent, wistfully
gazed astern.   When at last Pilgrim had been
hauled upon the railway levee, and the Doctor
and I had gone to summon a shipping clerk,
the lad looked pleadingly into W—'s face.
In tones half-choked with tears, he expressed
the sentiment of all: "Mother, is it really
ended ?   Why can't we go back to Brownsville, and do it all over again ?"

APPENDIX A.

Englishmen had no sooner set foot upon our
continent, than they began to penetrate inland
with the hope of soon reaching the Western
Ocean, which the coast savages, almost as
ignorant of the geography of the interior as
the Europeans themselves, declared lay just
beyond the mountains. In 1586, we find
Ralph Lane, governor of Raleigh's ill-fated
colony, leading his men up the Roanoke River
for a hundred miles, only to turn back dis-
heartened at the rapids and falls, which necessitated frequent portages through the forest
jungles. Twenty years later (1606), Christopher Newport and the redoubtable John Smith,
of Jamestown, ascended the James as far as
the falls—now Richmond, Va.; and Newport
himself, the following year, succeeded in reaching a point forty miles beyond, but here again
was appalled by the difficulties and returned.

There was, after this, a deal of brave talk about scaling the mountains; but nothing further was done until 1650, when Edward Bland and Edward Pennant again tried the Roanoke, though without penetrating the wilderness far beyond Lane's turning point. It is recorded that, in 1669, John Lederer, an adventurous German surgeon, commissioned as an explorer by Governor Berkeley, ascended to the summit of the Blue Ridge, in Madison County, Va.; but although he was once more on the spot the following season, with a goodly company of horsemen and Indians, and had a bird's-eye view of the over-mountain country, he does not appear to have descended into the world of woodland which lay stretched between him and the setting sun. It seems to be well established that the very next year (1671), a party under Abraham Wood, one of Governor Berkeley's major-generals, penetrated as far as the Great Falls of the Great Kanawha, only eighty miles from the Ohio—doubtless the first English exploration of waters flowing into the latter river. The Great Kanawha was, by Wood himself, called New River, but the geographers of the time styled it Wood's. The last title was finally dropped; the stream above the mouth of the Gauley is, however, still known as New. These several adventurers had now demonstrated that while the waters beyond the mountains were not the Western Ocean, they possibly led to such a sea; and it came to be recognized, too, that the continent was not as narrow as had up to this time been supposed.

Meanwhile, the French of Canada were casting eager eyes toward the Ohio, as a gateway to the continental interior. But the French-hating Iroquois held fast the upper waters of the Mohawk, Delaware, and Susquehanna, and the long but narrow watershed sloping northerly to the Great Lakes, so that the westering Ohio was for many years sealed to New France. An important factor in American history this, for it left the great valley practically free from whites while the English settlements were strengthening on the seaboard; when at last the French were ready aggressively to enter upon the coveted field, they had in the English colonists formidable and finally successful rivals.

It is believed by many, and the theory is not unreasonable, that the great French fur-trader and explorer, La Salle, was at the Falls

of the Ohio (site of Louisville) "in the autumn
or early winter of 1669." How he got there,
is another question. Some antiquarians believe that he reached the Alleghany by way
of the Chautauqua portage, and descended the
Ohio to the Falls; others, that he ascended
the Maumee from Lake Erie, and, descending
the Wabash, thus discovered the Ohio. It
was reserved for the geographer Franquelin to
give, in his map of 1688, the first fairly-accu-
rate idea of the Ohio's path; and Father Hen-
nepin's large map of 1697 showed that much
had meanwhile been learned about the river.

No doubt, by this time, the great waterway
was well-known to many of the most adventurous French and English fur-traders, possibly
better to the latter than to the former; unfor-
tunately, these men left few records behind
them, by which to trace their discoveries. As
early as 1684, we incidentally hear of the Ohio
as a principal route for the Iroquois, who
brought peltries "from the direction of the
Illinois" to the English at Albany, and the
French at Quebec. Two years after this, ten
English trading-canoes, loaded with goods,
were seen on Lake Erie by French agents,
who in great alarm wrote home to Quebec

about them. Writes De Nonville to Seignelay, "I consider it a matter of importance to preclude the English from this trade, as they doubtless would entirely ruin ours—as well by the cheaper bargains they would give the Indians, as by attracting to themselves the French of our colony who are in the habit of resorting to the woods."

Herein lay the gist of the whole matter: The legalized monopoly granted to the great fur-trade companies of New France, with the official corruption necessary to create and perpetuate that monopoly, made the French trade an expensive business, consequently goods were dear. On the other hand, the trade of the English was untrammeled, and a lively competition lowered prices. The French cajoled the Indians, and fraternized with them in their camps; whereas, the English despised the savages, and made little attempt to disguise their sentiments. The French, while claiming all the country west of the Alleghanies, cared little for agricultural colonization; they would keep the wilderness intact, for the fostering of wild animals, upon the trade in whose furs depended the welfare of New France—and this, too, was the policy of the savage. By

English statesmen at home, our continental interior was also chiefly prized for its forest trade, which yielded rich returns for the merchant adventurers of London. The policies of the English colonists and of their general government were ever clashing. The latter looked upon the Indian trade as an entering wedge; they thought of the West as a place for growth. Close upon the heels of the path-breaking trader, went the cattle-raiser, and, following him, the agricultural settler looking for cheap, fresh, and broader lands. No edicts of the Board of Trade could repress these backwoodsmen; savages could and did beat them back for a time, but the annals of the border are lurid with the bloody struggle of the borderers for a clearing in the Western forest. The greater part of them were Scotch-Irish from Pennsylvania, Virginia, the Carolinas—a hardy race, who knew not defeat. Steadily they pushed back the rampart of savagery, and won the Ohio valley for civiliza-ation.

The Indian early recognized the land-grabbing temper of the English, and felt that a struggle to the death was impending. The French browbeat their savage allies, and, easily inflaming their passions, kept the body of them almost continually at war with the English— the Iroquois excepted, not because the latter were English-lovers, or did not understand the aim of English colonization, but because the earliest French had won their undying enmity. Amidst all this weary strife, the Indian, a born trader who dearly loved a bargain, never failed to recognize that the goods of his French friends were dear, and that those of his enemies, the English, were cheap. We find frequent evidences that for a hundred years the tribesmen of the Upper Lakes carried on an illicit trade with the hated English, whenever the usually-wary French were thought to be napping.

It is certain that English forest traders were upon the Ohio in the year 1700. In 1715,— the year before Governor Spotswood of Virginia, "with much feasting and parade," made his famous expedition over the Blue Ridge,— there was a complaint that traders from Carolina had reached the villages on the Wabash, and were poaching on the French preserves. French military officers built little log stockades along that stream, and tried in vain to induce the Indians of the valley to remove to

St. Joseph's River, out of the sphere of English influence. Everywhere did French traders meet English competitors, who were not to be frightened by orders to move off the field. New France, therefore, determined to connect Canada and Louisiana by a chain of forts throughout the length of the Mississippi basin, which should not only secure untrammeled communication between these far-separated colonies, but aid in maintaining French supremacy throughout the region. Yet in 1725 we still hear of "the English from Carolina" busily trading with the Miamis under the very shadow of the guns of Fort Ouiatanon (near Lafayette, Ind.), and the French still vainly scolding thereat. What was going on upon the Wabash, was true elsewhere in the Ohio basin, as far south as the Creek towns on the sources of the Tennessee.

About this time, Pennsylvania and Virginia began to exhibit interest in their own overlapping claims to lands in the country northwest of the Ohio. Those colonies were now settled close to the base of the mountains, and there was heard a popular clamor for pastures new. French ownership of the over-mountain region was denied, and in 1728 Pennsylvania "viewed with alarm the encroachments of the French." The issue was now joined; both sides claimed the field, but, as usual, the contest was at first among the rival forest traders. In the Virginia and Pennsylvania capitals, the transmontane country was still a misty region. In 1729, Col. William Byrd, an authority on things Virginian, was able to write that nothing was then known in that colony of the sources of the Potomac, Roanoke, and Shenandoah. It was not until 1736 that Col. William Mayo, in laying out the boundaries of Lord Fairfax's generous estate, discovered in the Alleghanies the head-spring of the Potomac, where ten years later was planted the famous "Fairfax Stone," the southwest point of the boundary between Virginia and Maryland. That very same year (1746), M. de Léry, chief engineer of New France, went with a detachment of troops from Lake Erie to Chautauqua Lake, and proceeded thence by Conewango Creek and Alleghany River to the Ohio, which he carefully surveyed down to the mouth of the Great Miami.

Affairs moved slowly in those days. New France was corrupt and weak, and the English colonists, unaided by the home government, were not strong. For many years, nothing of importance came out of this rivalry of French and English in the Ohio Valley, save the petty quarrels of fur-traders, and the occasional adventure of some Englishman taken prisoner by Indians in a border foray, and carried far into the wilderness to meet with experiences the horror of which, as preserved in their published narratives, to this day causes the blood of the reader to curdle.

Now and then, there were voluntary adventurers into these strange lands. Such were John Howard, John Peter Salling, and two other Virginians who, the story goes, went overland (1740 or 1741) under commission of their inquisitive governor, to explore the country to the Mississippi. They went down Coal and Wood's Rivers to the Ohio, which in Salling's journal is called the "Alleghany." Finally, a party of French, negroes, and Indians took them prisoners and carried them to New Orleans, where on meager fare they were held in prison for eighteen months. They escaped at last, and had many curious adventures by land and sea, until they reached home, from

20

which they had been absent two years and three months. There are now few countries on the globe where a party of travelers could meet with adventures such as these.

At last, the plot thickened; the tragedy was hastened to a close. France now formally asserted her right to all countries drained by streams emptying into the St. Lawrence, the Great Lakes, and the Mississippi. This vast empire would have extended from the comb of the Rockies on the west—discovered in 1743 by the brothers La Vérendrye—to the crest of the Appalachians on the east, thus including the western part of New York and New England. The narrow strip of the Atlantic coast alone would have been left to the domination of Great Britain. The demand made by France, if acceded to, meant the death-blow to English colonization on the American mainland; and yet it was made not without reason. French explorers, missionaries, and fur-traders had, with great enterprise and fortitude, swarmed over the entire region, carrying the flag, the religion, and the commerce of France into the farthest forest wilds; while the colonists of their rival, busy in solidly welding their industrial commonwealths, had as yet scarcely peeped over the Alleghany barrier.

It was asserted on behalf of Great Britain, that the charters of her coast colonies carried their bounds far into the West; further, that as, by the treaty of Utrecht (1713), France had acknowledged the suzerainty of the British king over the Iroquois confederacy, the English were entitled to all lands ''conquered'' by those Indians, whose war-paths had extended from the Ottawa River on the north to the Carolinas on the south, and whose forays reached alike to the Mississippi and to New England. In this view was made, in 1744, the famous treaty at Lancaster, Pa., whereat the Iroquois, impelled by rum and presents, pretended to give to the English entire control of the Ohio Valley, under the claim that the former had in various encounters conquered the Shawanese of that region and were therefore entitled to it. It is obvious that a country occasionally raided by marauding bands of savages, whose homes are far away, cannot properly be considered theirs by conquest.

Meanwhile, both sides were preparing to occupy and hold the contested field. New France already had a weak chain of water-

side forts and commercial stations,—the rendezvous of fur-traders, priests, travelers, and
friendly Indians,—extending, with long intervening stretches of savage-haunted wilderness,
through the heart of the continent, from Lower
Canada to her outlying post of New Orleans.
It is not necessary here to enter into the details of the ensuing French and Indian War,
the story of which Parkman has told us so
well. Suffice it briefly to mention a few only
of its features, so far as they affect the Ohio
itself.

The Iroquois, although concluding with the
English this treaty of Lancaster, " on which,
as a corner-stone, lay the claim of the colonists
to the West," were by this time, as the result
of wily French diplomacy, growing suspicious
of their English protectors; at the same time,
having on several occasions been severely
punished by the French, they were less ran-
corous in their opposition to New France.
For this reason, just as the English were getting ready to make good their claim to the
Ohio by actual colonization, the Iroquois began
to let in the French at the back door. In
1749, Galissonière, then governor of New
France, dispatched to the great valley a party

of soldiers under Céloron de Bienville, with directions to conduct a thorough exploration, to bury at the mouths of principal streams lead plates graven with the French claim,—a custom of those days,—and to drive out English traders. Céloron proceeded over the Lake Chautauqua route, from Lake Erie to the Alleghany River, and thence down the Ohio to the Miami, returning to Lake Erie over the old Maumee portage. English traders, who could not be driven out, were found swarming into the country, and his report was discouraging. The French realized that they could not maintain connection between New Orleans and their settlements on the St. Lawrence, if driven from the Ohio valley. The governor sent home a plea for the shipment of ten thousand French peasants to settle the region; but the government at Paris was just then as indifferent to New France as was King George to his colonies, and the settlers were not sent.

Meanwhile, the English were not idle. The first settlement they made west of the mountains, was on New River, a branch of the Kanawha (1748); in the same season, several adventurous Virginians hunted and made land-

claims in Kentucky and Tennessee. Before
the close of the following year (1749), there
had been formed, for fur-trading and colonizing
purposes, the Ohio Company, composed of
wealthy Virginians, among whom were two
brothers of Washington. King George granted
the company five hundred thousand acres,
south of and along the Ohio River, on which
they were to plant a hundred families and
build and maintain a fort. As a base of supplies, they built a fortified trading-house at
Will's Creek (now Cumberland, Md.), near
the head of the Potomac, and developed a
trail ("Nemacolin's Path"), sixty miles long,
across the Laurel Hills to the mouth of Redstone Creek, on the Monongahela, where was
built another stockade (1752).

Christopher Gist, a famous backwoodsman,
was sent (1750), the year after Céloron's expedition, to explore the country as far down
as the falls of the Ohio, and select lands for
the new company. Gist's favorable report
greatly stimulated interest in the Western
country. In his travels, he met many Scotch-
Irish fur-traders who had passed into the West
through the mountain valleys of Pennsylvania,
Virginia, and the Carolinas. His negotiations

with the natives were of great value to the English cause.

It was early seen, by English and French alike, that an immense advantage would accrue to the nation first in possession of what is now the site of Pittsburg, the meeting-place of the Monongahela and Alleghany rivers to form the Ohio—the "Forks of the Ohio," as it was then called.   In the spring of 1753, a French force occupied the new fifteen-mile portage route between Presque Isle (Erie, Pa.) and French Creek, a tributary of the Alleghany. On the banks of French Creek they built Fort Le Bœuf, a stout log-stockade.   It had been planned to erect another fort at the Forks of the Ohio, one hundred and twenty miles below; but disease in the camp prevented the completion of the scheme.

What followed is familiar to all who have taken any interest whatever in Western history.   In November, Governor Dinwiddie, of Virginia, sent one of his major-generals, young George Washington, with Gist as a companion, to remonstrate with the French at Le Bœuf for occupying land "so notoriously known to be the property of the Crown of Great Britain." The French politely turned the messengers back. In the following April (1754), Washington set out with a small command, by the way of Will's Creek, to forcibly occupy the Forks. His advance party were building a fort there, when the French appeared and easily drove them off. Then followed Washington's defeat at Great Meadows (July 4). The French were now supreme at their new Fort Duquesne. The following year, General Braddock set out from Virginia, also by Nemacolin's Path; but, on that fateful ninth of July, fell in the slaughter-pen which had been set for him at Turtle Creek by the Indians of the Upper Lakes, under the leadership of a French fur-trader from far-off Wisconsin.

From the time of Braddock's defeat until the close of the war, French traders, with savage allies, poured the vials of their wrath upon the encroaching settlements of the English backwoodsmen. Nemacolin's Path, now known as Braddock's Road, made for the Indians of the Ohio an easy pathway to the English borders of Pennsylvania, Virginia, and Maryland. In the parallel valleys of the Alleghanies was waged a partisan warfare, which in bitterness has probably not had its equal in all the long history of the efforts of expanding civilization to beat down the encircling walls of barbarism. In 1758, Canada was attacked by several English expeditions, the most of which were successful. One of these was headed by General John Forbes, and directed against Fort Duquesne. After a remarkable forest march, overcoming mighty obstacles, Forbes arrived at his destination to find that the French had blown up the fortifications, some of the troops retreating to Lake Erie and others to rehabilitate Fort Massac on the Lower Ohio.

Thus England gained possession of the valley. New France had been cut in twain. The English Fort Pitt commanded the Forks of the Ohio, and French rule in America was now doomed. The fall of Quebec soon followed (1759), then of Montreal (1760); and in 1763 was signed the Treaty of Paris, by which England obtained possession of all the territory east of the Mississippi River, except the city of New Orleans and a small outlying district. In order to please the savages of the interior, and to cultivate the fur-trade,—perhaps also, to act as a check upon the westward growth of the too-ambitious coast colonies,— King George III. took early occasion to command his "loving subjects" in America not to purchase or settle lands beyond the mountains, "without our especial leave and license." It is needless to say that this injunction was not obeyed. The expansion of the English colonies in America was irresistible; the Great West was theirs, and they proceeded in due time to occupy it.

Long before the close of the French and Indian War, English colonists—whom we will now, for convenience, call Americans—had made agricultural settlements in the Ohio basin. As early as 1752, we have seen, the Redstone fort was built. In 1753, the French forces, on retiring from Great Meadows, burned several log cabins on the Monongahela. The interesting story of the colonizing of the Redstone district, at the western end of Braddock's Road, has been outlined in Chapter I. of the text; and it has been shown, in the course of the narrative of the pilgrimage, how other districts were slowly settled in the face of savage opposition. Although driven back in numerous Indian wars, these American borderers had come to the Ohio valley to stay.

We have seen the early attempt of the Ohio Company to settle the valley. Its agents blazed the way, but the French and Indian War, and the Revolution soon following, tended to discourage the aspirations of the adventurers, and the organization finally lapsed. Western land speculators were as active in those days as now, and Washington was chief among them. We find him first interested in the valley, through broad acres acquired on land-grants issued for military services in the French and Indian War; Revolutionary bounty claims made him a still larger landholder on Western waters; and, to the close of the century, he was actively interested in schemes to develop the region. We are not in the habit of so regarding him, but both by frequent personal presence in the Ohio valley, and extensive interests at stake there, the Father of his Country was the most conspicuous of Western pioneers. Dearly did Washington love the West, which he knew so well; when the Revolutionary cause looked dark, and it seemed possible that England might seize the coast settlements, he is said to have cried, "We will retire beyond the mountains, and be free!" and in his declining years he seemed to regret that he was too old to join his former comrades of the camp, in their colony at Marietta.

As early as 1754, Franklin, in his famous
Albany Plan of Union for the colonies, had a
device for establishing new states in the West,
upon lands purchased from the Indians. In
1773, he displayed interest in the Walpole
plan for another colony,—variously called
Pittsylvania, Vandalia, and New Barataria—
with its proposed capital at the mouth of the
Great Kanawha. There were, too, several
other Western colonial schemes, — among
them the Henderson colony of Transylvania,
between the Cumberland and the Tennessee,
the seat of which was Boonesborough. Read-
ers of Roosevelt well know its brief but brilliant career, intimately connected with the
development of Tennessee and Kentucky.
But the most of these hopeful enterprises came
to grief with the political secession of the
colonies; and when the coast States ceded
their Western land-claims to the new general
government, and the Ordinance of 1787 provided for the organization of the Territory
Northwest of the River Ohio, there was no
room for further enterprises of this character.*

---

* See Turner's "Western State-Making in the Revolution-
ary Era," in *Amer. Hist. Rev.*, Vol. I.; also, Alden's "New
Governments West of the Alleghanies," in *Bull. Univ. Wis.*,
Hist. Series, Vol. II.

The story of the Ohio is the story of the West. With the close of the Revolution, came a rush of travel down the great river. It was more or less checked by border warfare, which lasted until 1794; but in that year, Anthony Wayne, at the Battle of Fallen Timbers, broke the backbone of savagery east of the Mississippi; the Tecumseh uprising (1812-13) came too late seriously to affect the dwellers on the Ohio.

There were two great over-mountain highways thither, one of them being Braddock's Road, with Redstone (now Brownsville, Pa.) and Pittsburg as its termini; the other was Boone's old trail, or Cumberland Gap. With the latter, this sketch has naught to do.

By the close of the Revolution, Pittsburg— in Gist's day, but a squalid Indian village, and a fording-place—was still only "a distant outpost, merely a foothold in the Far West." By 1785, there were a thousand people there, chiefly engaged in the fur-trade and in forwarding emigrants and goods to the rapidly-growing settlements on the middle and lower reaches of the river. The population had doubled by 1803. By 1812 there was to be seen here just the sort of bustling, vicious

frontier town, with battlement-fronts and ragged streets, which Buffalo and then Detroit
became in after years.   Cincinnati and Chicago, St. Louis and Kansas City, had still
later, each in turn, their share of this experience; and, not many years ago, Bismarck,
Omaha, and Leadville.   From Philadelphia
and Baltimore and Richmond, there were running to Pittsburg or Redstone regular lines of
stages for the better class of passengers; freight
wagons laden with immense bales of goods
were to be seen in great caravans, which frequently were ''stalled'' in the mud of the
mountain roads; emigrants from all parts of
the Eastern States, and many countries of
Europe, often toiled painfully on foot over
these execrable highways, with their bundles
on their backs, or following scrawny cattle
harnessed to makeshift vehicles; and now and
then came a well-to-do equestrian with his
pack-horses, —generally an Englishman,—who
was out to see the country, and upon his return to write a book about it.

   At Pittsburg, and points on the Alleghany,
Youghiogheny, and Monongahela, were boat-
building yards which turned out to order a
curious medley of craft—arks, flat- and keel-

boats, barges, pirogues, and schooners of
every design conceivable to fertile brain.
Upon these, travelers took passage for the then
Far West, down the swift-rolling Ohio. There
have descended to us a swarm of published
journals by English and Americans alike, giving pictures, more or less graphic, of the men
and manners of the frontier; none is without
interest, even if in its pages the priggish author but unconsciously shows himself, and
fails to hold the mirror up to the rest of nature. With the introduction of steamboats,—
the first was in 1811, but they were slow to
gain headway against popular prejudice,—the
old river life, with its picturesque but rowdy
boatmen, its unwieldy flats and keels and
arks, began to pass away, and water traffic to
approach the prosaic stage; the crossing of
the mountains by the railway did away with
the boisterous freighters, the stages, and the
coaching-taverns; and when, at last, the river
became paralleled by the iron way, the glory
of the steamboat epoch itself faded, riverside
towns adjusted themselves to the new highways
of commerce, new centers arose, and "side-
tracked" ports fell into decay.

APPENDIX B.

Selected list of Journals of previous travelers down the Ohio.

Gist, Christopher. Gist's Journals; with historical, geographical, and ethnological notes, and biographies of his contemporaries, by William M. Darlington. Pittsburg, 1893.

Gist's trip down the valley, from October, 1750, to May, 1751, was on horseback, as far as the site of Frankfort, Ky. On his second trip into Kentucky, from November, 1751, to March 11, 1752, he touched the river at few points.

Gordon, Harry. Extracts from the Journal of Captain Harry Gordon, chief engineer in the Western department in North America, who was sent from Fort Pitt, on the River Ohio, down the said river, etc., to Illinois, in 1766.

Published in Pownall's "Topographical Description of North America," Appendix, p. 2.

Washington, George. Journal of a tour to the Ohio River. [Writings, ed. by Ford, vol. II. New York, 1889.]

The trip lasted from October 5 to December 1, 1770. The

party went in boats from Fort Pitt, as far down as the mouth of the Great Kanawha. This journal is the best on the subject, written in the eighteenth century.

Pownall, T. A topographical description of such parts of North America as are contained in the [annexed] map of the Middle British Colonies, etc.   London, 1776.

Contains "Extracts from Capt. Harry Gordon's Journal," "Extracts from Mr. Lewis Evans' Journal" of 1743, and "Christopher Gist's Journal" of 1750-51.

Hutchins, Thomas. Topographical description of Virginia, Pennsylvania, Maryland, and North Carolina, comprehending the Rivers Ohio, Kenhawa, Sioto, Cherokee, Wabash, Illinois, Mississippi, etc.   London, 1778.

St. John, M. Lettres d'un cultivateur Americain.   Paris, 1787, 3 vols.

Vol. 3 contains an account of the author's boat trip down the river, in 1784.

De Vigni, Antoine F. S. Relation of his voyage down the Ohio River from Pittsburg to the Falls, in 1788.

Graphic and animated account by a French physician who came out with the Scioto Company's immigrants to Gallipolis.   Given in "Proc. Amer. Antiq. Soc.", Vol. XI., pp. 369-380.

May, John. Journal and letters [to the Ohio country, 1788-89].   Cincinnati, 1873.

One of the best, for economic views. May was a Boston merchant.

21

Forman, Samuel S.   Narrative of a journey down the Ohio and Mississippi in 1789-90. With a memoir and illustrative notes, by Lyman C. Draper.   Cincinnati, 1888.

A lively and appreciative account. Touches social life at the garrisons, *en route*.

Ellicott, Andrew.   Journal of the late commissioner on behalf of the United States during part of the year 1796, the years 1797, 1798, 1799, and part of the year 1800: for determining the boundary between the United States and Spain.   Philadelphia, 1803.

His trip down the river was in 1796.

Baily, Francis.   Journal of a tour in unsettled parts of North America, in 1796 and 1797.   London, 1856.

The author's river voyage was in 1796.

Harris, Thaddeus Mason.   Journal of a tour into the territory northwest of the Alleghany Mountains; made in the spring of the year 1803.   Boston, 1805.

A valuable work. The author traveled on a flatboat.

Michaux, F. A.   Travels to the west of the Alleghany Mountains.   London (2nd ed.), 1805.

Excellent, for economic conditions. The expedition was made in 1802.

Ashe, Thomas. Travels in America, performed in 1806. London, 1808.

Among the best of the early journals, although abounding in exaggerations.

Cuming, F. Sketches of a tour to the Western country, etc., commenced in 1807 and concluded in 1809. Pittsburg, 1810.

Bradbury, John. Travels [1809-11] in the interior of America. Liverpool, 1817.

Melish, John. Travels in the United States of America [1811]. Philadelphia, 1812, 2 vols.

Vol. 2 contains the journal of the author's voyage down the river, in a skiff. The account of means of early navigation is graphic.

Flint, Timothy. Recollections of the last ten years. Boston, 1826.

There is no better account of boats, and river life generally, in 1814-15, the time of Flint's voyage.

Fearon, Henry Bradshaw. Sketches of America [1817]. London, 1819.

Palmer, John. Journal of travels in the United States of North America [1817]. London, 1818.

Evans, Estwick. A pedestrian tour [1818] of four thousand miles through the Western states and territories. Concord, N. H., 1819.

Birkbeck, Morris. Notes on a journey in

America, from the coast of Virginia to the Territory of Illinois. London, 1818.

The author traveled, in 1817, by light wagon from Richmond to Pittsburg; and from Pittsburg to Cincinnati by horseback. This book, interesting for economic conditions, together with the author's "Letters from Illinois," did much to inspire emigration to Illinois from England. His English colony, at English Prairie, Ill., was much visited by travelers of the period.

Faux, W. Journal of a tour to the United States [in 1819].

Excellent pictures of American life and agricultural methods, by an English gentleman farmer. Attacks Birkbeck's roseate views.

Ogden, George W. Letters from the West, comprising a tour through the Western country [1821], and a residence of two summers in the States of Ohio and Kentucky. New Bedford, Mass., 1823.

Welby, Adlard. A visit to North America and the English settlements in Illinois. London, 1821.

The author went by horseback, occasionally touching the river towns.

Beltrami, J. C. Pilgrimage in Europe and America. London, 1828, 2 vols.

In Vol. II the author describes a steamboat journey in 1823, from Pittsburg to the mouth.

Hall, James. Letters from the West. London, 1828.

Valuable for scenery, manners, and customs, and anecdotes of early Western settlement.

Anonymous. The Americans as they are; described by a tour through the valley of the Mississippi. London, 1828.

Trollope, Mrs. [Frances M.]. Domestic manners of the Americans. London and New York, 1832.

A lively caricature, the precursor of Dickens' "American Notes." Mrs. Trollope's voyages on the Ohio were in 1828 and 1830.

Vigne, Godfrey T. Six months in America. London, 1832, 2 vols.

Hamilton, T. Men and manners in America. Philadelphia, 1833.

Includes a steamboat journey from Pittsburg to New Orleans.

Alexander, Capt. J. E. Transatlantic sketches. London, 1833, 2 vols.

Vol. II. has an account of a trip up the river.

Stuart, James. Three years in North America. New York, 1833, 2 vols.

Vol. II. includes a voyage up the Ohio. The author takes issue, throughout, with Mrs. Trollope.

Brackenridge, H. M. Recollections of persons and places in the West.   Philadelphia, 1834.

Describes river trips, during the first decade of the century.

Tudor, Henry.   Narrative of a tour [1831-32] in North America.   London, 1834, 2 vols.

The Ohio trip is in Vol. II.

Arfwedson, C. D.   The United States and Canada, in 1832, 1833, and 1834.   London, 1834, 2 vols.

In Vol. II is a report of a steamboat trip up the river.

Latrobe, Charles Joseph.   The rambler in North America.   New York, 1835, 2 vols.

Vol. I1 has an account of a descending steamboat voyage.

Anonymous.   A winter in the West.   By a New Yorker.   New York (2nd ed.), 1835, 2 vols.

In Vol. I. is an entertaining account of a stage-coach ride in 1833, from Pittsburg to Cleveland, touching all settlements on the Upper Ohio down to Beaver River.

Nichols, Thomas L.   Forty years of American life.   London, 1864, 2 vols.

In Vol. I. the author tells of a steamboat tour from Pittsburg to New Orleans, in 1840.

Dickens, Charles.   American notes.   New York, 1842.

Dickens, in 1841, traveled in steamboats from Pittsburg to St. Louis. His dyspeptic comments on life and manners in the United States, at the time grated harshly on the ears of our people; but afterward, they grew strong and wise enough to smile at them. The book is to-day, like Mrs. Trollope's, entertaining reading for an American.

Rubio (pseud.). Rambles in the United States and Canada, in 1845. London, 1846.

A typical English growler, who thinks America "the most disagreeable of all disagreeable countries;" nevertheless, he says of the Ohio, "a finer thousand miles of river scenery could hardly be found in the wide world."

Mackay, Alex. The Western world; or, travels in the United States in 1846-47. London, 1849.

Good for its character sketches, glimpses of slavery, and report of economic conditions.

Robertson, James. A few months in America [winter of 1853-54]. London, n. d.

Chiefly statistical.

Murray, Charles Augustus. Travels in North America. London, 1854, 2 vols.

Vol. I has the Ohio-river trip. The author is an appreciative Englishman, and tells his story well.

Murray, Henry A. Lands of the slave and the free. London, 1855, 2 vols.

In Vol. I is an account of an Ohio-river voyage.

Ferguson, William. America by river and rail [in 1855]. London, 1856.

Lloyd, James T. Steamboat directory, and disasters on the Western waters. Cincinnati, 1856.

Valuable for stories and records of the early days of river transportation.

Anonymous. A short American tramp in the fall of 1864. By the editor of " Life in Normandy." Edinburgh, 1865.

An English geologist's journal. Distorted and overdrawn, on the travel side. He took steamer from St. Louis to Cincinnati.

Bishop, Nathaniel H. Four months in a sneak-box. Boston, 1879.

The author, in the winter of 1875-76, voyaged in an open boat from Pittsburg to New Orleans, and along the Gulf coast to Florida.

INDEX.

329

Shawnee Classics
A Series of Classic Regional Reprints for the Midwest

Personal Memoirs of John H. Brinton
Civil War Surgeon, 1861–1865
John H. Brinton

Stagecoach and Tavern Tales of the Old Northwest
Harry Ellsworth Cole
Edited by Louise Phelps Kellogg

The Great Cyclone at St. Louis and East St. Louis, May 27, 1896
Compiled and Edited by Julian Curzon

A Knight of Another Sort
Prohibition Days and Charlie Birger
Gary DeNeal

"Black Jack"
John A. Logan and Southern Illinois in the Civil War Era
James Pickett Jones

Reminiscences of a Soldier's Wife
An Autobiography
Mrs. John A. Logan

Before Mark Twain
A Sampler of Old, Old Times on the Mississippi
Edited by John Francis McDermott

History 31st Regiment Illinois Volunteers
Organized by John A. Logan
W. S. Morris, L. D. Hartwell, and J. B. Kuykendall

**A History of the Ninth Regiment Illlinois Volunteer
Infantry, with the Regimental Roster**
Marion Morrison

Tales and Songs of Southern Illinois
Collected by Charles Neely
Edited with a Foreword by John Webster Spargo

The Outlaws of Cave-in-Rock
Otto A. Rothert

A Woman's Story of Pioneer Illinois
Christiana Holmes Tillson
Edited by Milo Milton Quaife

Army Life of an Illinois Soldier
Including a Day-by-Day Record of Sherman's March
to the Sea
Charles W. Wills